Oval House Theatre, BEcreativ

FIXER

BY
LYDIA ADETUNJI

**A new version of *Fixer* was produced at Oval House Theatre
on Tuesday 21 June 2011**

Fixer was first produced at the HighTide Festival in 2009.
The play was developed with the support of the Almeida Theatre.

FIXER

BY
LYDIA ADETUNJI

Cast

SARA	Jennifer Jackson
LAURENCE	Damola Adelaja
PORTER	Nick Oshikanlu
CHUKS	Richard Pepple
DAVE	Alex Barclay
JEROME	Robert Bowman
TRACKSUIT MAN	Babajide Fado

Creative Team

Directors	Dan Barnard and Rachel Briscoe
Production Designer	Chris Gylee
Lighting Designer	Arnim Friess
Composer & Sound Designer	Richard Hammarton
Costume Supervisor	Bianca Ward
Assistant Designer	Philippa Thomas
Production Manager	Bernd Fauler
Deputy Stage Manager	Suu Wernham
Assistant Stage Manager	Sylvia Darkwa-Ohemeng
Production Assistant	Sarah Crompton
fanSHEN Production Assistant	Lou Glover
Publicity Design	Lulu Kitololo (asilia)

Production Acknowledgements

Ben Amunwa, ArtsAdmin, Claire Birch, Christine Buckly, Brian Cathcart, CCMS for cleaning services, Joseph Croft, Nathan Curry, Elizabeth Donnelly, Matt Drury at the Royal Court, Caroline Duffield, English Touring Theatre, Gabriel Gatehouse, Barbara Gordon, Adam Higazi, Lucy Kerbel, Kirsty McQuire, Kathryn Nwajiaku-Dahou, Paul at Sparks, Tom Parry, Dipo Salimonu, Richard Smith, Claire Tauban, Michelle Thompson, Jennifer Wallace, Ruth Watson, World Development Movement.

Lydia Adetunji would like to thank the Almeida theatre and Jinny McAllister Playwriting Fund, the HighTide Festival, Tanya Tillett and Sam Coates for their help in the development of this play.

Chris Hondros, Photojournalist (1970–2011)
fanSHEN and Oval House would like to acknowledge the inspiring work of Chris Hondros, award-winning photojournalist. Chris gave us permission to use his incredible image of Dagogo Joel shortly before he was killed in Libya , on 20 April 2011, while documenting the impact of the civil war on the lives of normal Libyans.

Producers

Oval House is a local theatre for an international city dedicated to staging brave new work by artists who are too uncompromising for the mainstream. We present theatre that is relevant to the UK's cosmopolitan capital and, reflecting contemporary London, Oval's programme is increasingly international in focus. We champion stories that you will not hear anywhere else and invest in exploration and development, inspiring artists to challenge themselves to become the world-class theatre-makers of tomorrow.

BEcreative develops and presents theatre in London, the UK, and abroad – making international theatre for a local audience. Led by Creative Director, Ben Evans, BEcreative offers bespoke artistic and managerial support to risk-taking theatre-makers challenging the mainstream.

fanSHEN tells stories of real people exploring big questions. We seek to challenge, confound and surprise. We make shows that grow locally but exist in dialogue with international traditions of theatre. Our work is co-directed, enabling us to combine the psychological detail of a character-focused process with the dynamic aesthetics of an audience-led approach. In 2010, our fifth birthday year, we won one award, made two and a half shows, and reached 3500 audience members.

Cast

Damola Adelaja – LAURENCE
Nigerian-born Damola Adelaja is a recent graduate of the Royal Academy of Dramatic Art. Productions at RADA include: *Three Sisters* (dir. Sir Jonathan Miller), Raz Shaw's *Hortensia and the Museum of Dreams*, and Toby Frow's *The Last Days of Judas Iscariot*. Since leaving RADA, he has appeared in *A Raisin in the Sun* (Royal Exchange, Manchester); *Ruined* (Almeida); and *Slave* (Lowry). This year Damola appeared in *Cornwell Estate* for BBC Radio, on television on BBC's *Doctors* as well as workshops at the National Theatre Studio and Tiata Fahodzi. Damola is passionate about theatre that has a political slant, a running motif in many of the plays he has appeared in. He is currently developing his very first play, a period piece set in Nigeria.

Alex Barclay – DAVE
Alex trained at Guildhall. Theatre includes: *As You Like It, The Tempest* and *Twelfth Night* (Sprite/York Theatre Royal); *Richard III* and *Accidental Death of an Anarchist* (Love and Madness tour); *Stage Fright* (Canal Café); *Bloody Poetry* (Cara Luna, White Bear); *Dead Dog at the Dry Cleaners* and *The Empire Builders* (Pleasance, London); and *Private Lives* (Iceni). He is an ongoing collaborator with The Factory, Coney, and Actors for Human Rights. Film includes: *The Queen's Sister* (Touchstone/Channel 4); Stephen Fry's *Bright Young Things*; and Luc Besson's *The Lady*.

Robert Bowman – JEROME
Theatre includes: *An Inspector Calls* (National Theatre and tour); *Haroun and the Sea of Stories* (National Theatre); *Twelfth Night, The Wives' Excuse* and *The Broken Heart* (RSC). He was a member of the Young Vic Ensemble appearing in *Grimm Tales* and *More Grimm Tales, The Comedy of Errors* (RSC/Young Vic); *As I Lay Dying* and *Twelfth Night*. Other theatre includes: Reverend Hale in *The Crucible* (RSC/Gielgud); the title role in *Cyrano De Bergerac* (Bristol Old Vic); Sherman Cymru's *Deep Cut* (Edinburgh Fringe/Tricycle); *The Orestia, Ivanov* (National Theatre); *Spinning into Butter* (Royal Court); *Love in a Wood* and *The Prisoner's Dilemma* (RSC); and *The Nest* (Living Pictures). Robert was Artistic Associate at the Bristol Old Vic for 2007 and is Joint Artistic Director of Living Pictures Productions. He teaches acting at Trinity College, Carmarthen.

Babajide Fado – TRACKSUIT MAN

Babajide Fado was born in Nigeria and moved to England at the age of ten. He received a DADA scholarship to train at Drama Studio, London, graduating in 2009. Roles whilst training include: Lord Foppington in *The Relapse*, Larry in *Closer* and Astrov in *Uncle Vanya*. Recent theatre includes: *The Lion and the Unicorn/Moving Tales* (Eastern Angles tour); *A Midsummer Night's Dream* (T.Atrica); and *Fair Trade* (Shatterbox Theatre Company, London and Edinburgh).

Jennifer Jackson – SARA

Jennifer trained at the East 15 Acting School, graduating in 2007. Theatre includes: *Amphibians* (Offstage Theatre/Bridewell); *Remote Control* (Tangled Feet); *Blowing* (Company of Angels and fanSHEN); *The Condor and the Maiden* (King's Head); *The Doorbells of Florence* (Tom Wright at Rosemary Branch); *Moshing Lying Down* (fanSHEN at Arcola and Shunt Vaults); *The Kathy Acker Mobile Library* (Ben Webb at Canal Café); *The Bitter Tears of Petra von Kant* (Yvonne McDevitt at Shunt Vaults); and Marya in *The Government Inspector* (Exeter Northcott). Jennifer is also co-artistic director of Running Bare Theatre, whose first show *Your Polar Bear* played at festivals last summer and at the Shunt Yard.

Nick Oshikanlu – PORTER

Nick rained at Guildhall School of Music and Drama. Theatre includes: *Iya-Ile, The Estate, The Gods are not to Blame* all with Tiata Fahodzi; *Bulletproof Soul* (Birmingham Rep); *My Home* (London Bubble); *Crocodile Seeking Refuge* (Lyric Hammersmith); *National Alien Office* (Riverside Studios); *References to Salvador Dali Make me Hot, Gompers* (Arcola). Television includes: *Cop School* (CBBC), *Holby City, Silent Witness, Little Miss Jocelyn*. Radio includes: *A Long Journey, Preserved of God*. As a director, Nick has directed *Pandora's Box* and worked as Assistant Director on *Joe Guy*.

Richard Pepple – CHUKS

Richard trained at Arts Educational Schools, London. Theatre includes: *Septimus Severus* (Collective Artists/Oval House); *The Estate, 365 Plays/365 Days* (Tiata Fahodzi); *Full Circle* (fanSHEN/Oval House); *Coriolanus* (RSC); *Baghdad Othello* reading (Tricycle); White Open Spaces (Pentabus); *The Burial* (Almeida); *The Hounding of David Oluwale* (West Yorkshire Playhouse and tour); *Medea, Medea* (Gate/Headlong). Workshops include: *The Coat* and more recently *Congo Iliad* (National Theatre Studio), and *Blowing* (fanSHEN). Television and film includes: *Nathan Barley* (Channel 4); *The Bill* (Talkback Thames); *Shoot the Messenger* (BBC2); *Caught in a Trap* (ITV); *No Ordinary Trifle* (Trifle Films Ltd). Radio includes: *The Estate* (BBC World Drama); *Revenge of the Celebrity Mums* (BBC R7); *A Second Night to Midnight* (BBC Drama North); *Next of Kin* (BBC R4).

Creative Team

Lydia Adetunji – Writer
Having previously worked in journalism, Lydia won the Almeida Theatre's 'Write' competition in 2006, and subsequently completed attachments to the Royal Court, National Theatre Studio, and Paines Plough, where she was Pearson Playwright-in-Residence. An earlier version of *Fixer* was performed at the HighTide Festival in Suffolk in 2009, was chosen as an outstanding example of international theatre at the National Play Festival in Brisbane, 2010, and was nominated for the Meyer-Whitworth Award. Other work has included *Floor 44* and *Trickster*, both produced at the Young Vic as part of ATC's Play Size, *Canton Kitty*, performed at Shakespeare's Globe, and *Hot*, a site-specific piece for Oval House Theatre. She was commissioned by Oràn Mór in Glasgow to write a play for the 'Play, Pie and a Pint' season. Lydia wrote a short play as part of the Tricycle Theatre's *Women, Power and Politics* season and a new full-length commission for the same theatre. Lydia's noir script *Necropolis* was fourth on the 2008 Brit List, an industry poll of the best unproduced screenplays in the country, and is now under option to Stealth Films. She is also developing an original screenplay with Cowboy Films and BBC Films.

Dan Barnard – Co-director
Dan is artistic director of fanSHEN Theatre Company. For fanSHEN he has co-directed *Blowing* by Jeroen van den Berg (national tour); *Moshing Lying Down* by Marcelo dos Santos (Shunt and tour) and *Shooting Rats* by Peter Turrini (Lilian Baylis Old Site) and directed *Meetings* by Mustapha Matura (Arcola). Dan's freelance directing work includes *Three Way* by Yusra Warsama (Birmingham Rep) and *Colors* by Peca Stefan (Tristan Bates, co-directed with Rachel Briscoe). Work as assistant director includes *Jerusalem* by Jez Butterworth (Apollo). In the Autumn Dan will co-direct *Same Same* by Shireen Mula for fanSHEN at Oval House Theatre.

Rachel Briscoe – Co-director
Rachel is creative director of fanSHEN. For fanSHEN, she has co-directed *Blowing* (national tour); *Moshing Lying Down* (Shunt, PULSE, festivals tour) and *Shooting Rats* (Lilian Baylis site); and directed *Full Circle* (Oval House). Freelance directing includes *Colors* by Peca Stefan (Tristan Bates, co-directed with Dan Barnard); *Inches Apart* (Winner of the Old Vic New Voices Theatre503 Award); *As Vingadoras* (a clown version of The Avengers with Galician company Maquinaria Pesada). In October, Rachel will co-direct Shireen Mula's *Same Same* for fanSHEN at Oval House Theatre.

Sarah Crompton – Production Assistant
Sarah is a freelance producer, currently working in London and Cambridge. She has been working on the stage and behind the scenes since she was young, but moved into producing theatre three years ago. Since then she has worked with Gecko Theatre Company (Assistant Producer of *The Overcoat*), State of Emergency Dance Company (Co-tour Manager), Shatterbox (Producer of *Fair Trade*), and is currently producing *Romeo and Juliet* for Night Light Theatre Company in Cambridge.

Sylvia Darkwa-Ohemeng – Assistant Stage Manager
Sylvia is in her third year currently studying at Rose Bruford College doing a BA (Hons) degree in Stage Management. She has been freelancing at Oval House since August, working on shows including *Estate Walls* by Arinze Kene. She was also heavily involved in the 33% London Festival working as one of the stage managers. She has also worked at the Cochrane Theatre, Unicorn Theatre and the Playhouse Theatre, Embankment, and festivals like SouthWestFest. She is hoping to increase her skills within the profession and travel within her career.

Arnim Friess – Lighting Designer
Arnim trained and worked as a photographer and audio-visual media designer in his native Germany, before moving to the UK to study Scenography, receiving an MA at Birmingham Institute of Art and Design. He is the founder member of Pixelbox Ltd, which specialises in designing dynamic performance environments, blending media like lighting, slide and video projection, animation, film-making and graphic design. Recent designs include: *Ghosts in the Walls* (RSC); *The Rememberers* (Birmingham REP and Apples&Snakes); *We Love You City* (Talking Birds at Belgrade). Past designs include: science-fiction opera *The Pitchshifter* for leading Dutch contemporary music ensemble Insomnia, award-winning *Rumblefish*, bricks-in-space spectacle *Life on Mars* (Legolands worldwide).

Bernd Fauler – Production Manager
Bernd enjoys working as a freelance production manager on a variety of projects, including contemporary performance/live art, theatre and dance as well as outdoor performances. Credits include: Sacred 2009/2010, a Season of Contemporary Performance (Chelsea); *That's the Way to Do It* (Red Herring Productions); *Access All Areas* (Live Art Development Agency); *Gross Indecency* (Duckie); *Hurts Given And Received / Slowly* (Howard Barker Season 2010 at Riverside Studios); *Soulplay, Kate Flatt Projects, Where's My Desi Soulmate, It Ain't All Bollywood, Meri Christmas, The Deranged Marriage* (Rifco Arts).

Lou Glover – fanSHEN Production Assistant

Lou Glover is an independant arts professional specialising in project management, front of house/venue management and events co-ordination. Recent projects include working on fanSHEN and Company of Angels' UK tour of *Blowing*, developing and delivering a Leadership In Philanthropy workshop for high-net-worth individuals, project managing the Pleasance Kidzone at a new classical music festival, as well as working in the operations department at the Roundhouse. Over the last ten years Lou has also been involved with Pleasance Islington and Edinburgh, artsdepot, Riverside Studios, the Roundhouse and Institute for Philanthropy. Lou holds an MA in Arts Administration and Cultural Policy from Goldsmiths and a BSc Hons in Sociology from LSE.

Chris Gylee – Designer

Chris trained at Bristol Old Vic Theatre School and was a selected designer on Cheek by Jowl's inaugural Young Director/Designer programme. For Shakespeare at the Tobacco Factory, Bristol, he has designed *Hamlet*, *The Taming of the Shrew*, *Othello* and *Much Ado About Nothing*. Other plays include: *Henry V* (Southwark Playhouse); *Colörs*, *Tattoo* (Company of Angels); *Grimms – The Final Chapter* (Trafalgar Studios); *Not Knowing Who We Are* (Blue Elephant); and designs for Arts Ed, Theatre503, Bristol Old Vic, and the Jermyn Street Theatre. Site-specific designs include: *Fanshen* (Theatre Delicatessen); *Shooting Rats* (fanSHEN); *Oliver Twist* (the egg). Chris is an associate designer with Fairground for whom he designed *The Red Man*, *Out of Touch* and *Bonnie & Clyde*. Chris's work as an illustrator and artist includes performance collaborations with Bristol Ferment.

Richard Hammarton – Composer & Sound Designer

Theatre includes: *Dr Faustus* (Royal Exchange, Manchester); *Speaking in Tongues* (Duke of Yorks); *Ghosts* (Duchess); *People at Sea*, *The Real Thing*, *Arsenic and Old Lace*, *Les Liaisons Dangereuses*, *The Constant Wife* (Salisbury Playhouse); *Pride and Prejudice* (Bath Theatre Royal and national tour); *The Mountaintop* (Trafalgar 1/Theatre503); *Breakfast With Mugabe* (Bath Ustinov); *Some Kind of Bliss*, *World's End*, *Hello and Goodbye* (Trafalgar Studios); *The Rise and Fall of Little Voice* (Harrogate). TV/Film composition includes: *Agatha Christie's Marple* (series 3 and 4), *The Secret of Chimneys* (ITV); *Wipeout* (children's drama); *Sex 'n' Death* (BBC); *Rajan and his Evil Hypnotist* (Channel 4). TV/Film orchestration includes *Primeval*, *Jericho*, *Agatha Christie's Marple* (series 1 & 2); *The Nine Lives of Tomas Katz* (UK Feature Films).

Philippa Thomas – Assistant Designer
After studying illustration at Edinburgh College of Art, Philippa decided to make the move into the world of performance with a masters in Set and Costume Design at the Bristol Old Vic Theatre School two years ago. Since graduating she has enjoyed working with a variety of companies and practitioners in theatre, film, festival and events. She is living and working in Bristol and is currently happy to find herself at Oval House Theatre for the first time.

Bianca Ward – Costume Supervisor
Bianca Ward trained at Bristol Old Vic Theatre School. Previously having studied Textiles at Central Saint Martins, she has now honed her skills to incorporate textiles into her costume practice. Recently she has co-designed costumes and supervised a show with Edward Sharpe and the Magnetic Zeros at the Old Vic Tunnels. At Christmas she supervised *Pinocchio* at the Tobacco Factory, Bristol, and has made for and assisted the recent Shakespeare season there. As well as supervising this year she also made costumes for BBC period drama *32 Brinkburn Street* and for *Thriller the Musical*.

Suu Wernham – Deputy Stage Manager
Suu began her career working as a sound engineer at the London Palladium on *The King and I*, *Barnum* and *Singing in the Rain*. Following this she spent several years with the Royal Shakespeare Company at the Barbican before returning to stage management and touring with companies such as the Reduced Shakespeare Company, the Young Vic, and English Touring Theatre. Having recently spent time in the USA developing projects with theatre companies and musicians, she hopes to continue this work in the future.

Since the 1960s, Oval House Theatre has been a pioneering supporter of queer, feminist and ethnically diverse performance work and we remain committed to exploding preconceptions of what theatre is and can be.

Today, Oval House is a local theatre for an international city dedicated to staging brave new work by artists who are too uncompromising for the mainstream. We work with the most exciting companies from London, the UK and beyond to present theatre that is relevant to the UK's cosmopolitan capital.

We champion stories that you will not hear anywhere else and invest in exploration and development, inspiring artists to challenge themselves to become the world-class theatre-makers of tomorrow.

Autumn 2011 at Oval House Theatre

We open with an explosion of Latin American culture: the return of CASA Festival brings us the very best of contemporary hispanic performance.

Autumn at Oval House Theatre sees a Lady-Led season filled with the bold new voices of some of the UK's most exciting female theatre-makers.

We present two incredible new plays by two distinctive playwrights. Stacey Gregg's *Lagan* and Shireen Mula's *Same Same* subvert familiar theatrical forms to tell compelling stories of longing and belonging.

Stella Duffy returns to Oval House with Shaky Isles and their story of sea monsters in the London sewers: *Taniwha Thames*.

Following a sellout work in progress showing as part of our TRANSGRESSIONS season, we welcome back Mars.tarrab with *Tomboy Blues: The Theory of Disappointment* for more disappointment, more theories and more culottes.

See you in the autumn.

Oval House Theatre   **Tel: 020 7582 0080**
52-54 Kennington Oval   **Fax: 020 7820 0990**
London   **info@ovalhouse.com**
SE11 5SW   **www.ovalhouse.com**

Oval House Theatre

Oval House Theatre and the London via Lagos festival gratefully acknowledge financial
support from Arts Council England, Lambeth Arts, London Councils, The Morel
Charitable Trust, The Steel Charitable Trust, The Gibbs Charitable Trust, Unity Theatre
Trust, The 8th Earl of Sandwich Memorial Trust, Grange Farm Trust, the Royal Victoria Hall
Foundation, The Peter Brook Mark Marvin Rent Subsidy Award and Barry Cox.

Photos by: Robert Day and Richard Hubert Smith

surprise • delight • enrich • engage

Under the directorship of Rachel Tackley, ETT presents potent, vivid and vital productions of new and classic plays to audiences far and wide. A powerhouse of touring theatre, ETT works with a rich and varied mix of the country's leading directors, actors and artists to stage thrilling and ambitious theatre that is vigorous, popular and, above all, entertaining.

Supported by
ARTS COUNCIL ENGLAND

www.ett.org.uk

FIXER

Lydia Adetunji

Characters

PILOT, *voice-over*

SARA, *British, twenties*

LAURENCE, *Black-British, twenties*

PORTER, *Nigerian, twenties–thirties*

CHUKS, *Nigerian, thirties*

DAVE, *British, thirties*

JEROME, *American, thirties*

MAN IN FLIP-FLOPS, *Nigerian, thirties*

MAN IN MIRROR SHADES, *Nigerian, twenties–thirties*

TRACKSUIT MAN, *Nigerian, thirties*

STEWARDESS, *voice-over*

The following roles can be doubled:
PORTER / MAN IN MIRROR SHADES
TRACKSUIT MAN / MAN IN FLIP-FLOPS

This text went to press before the end of rehearsals and so may differ slightly from the play as performed.

2

Scene One

Two airline seats, adjacent but spaced as if with an aisle between. LAURENCE *sits in one. He has a pair of large headphones in his lap, but he is listening to* SARA, *who is in the other seat. She is animated, drink in hand.*

PILOT (*over speaker*). Ladies and gentlemen, this is your captain speaking. We will shortly be at our maximum cruising altitude of 43,000 feet, which we will maintain until we begin our descent into Lagos approximately five hours from now.

SARA. No, no. I'm a fireman.

LAURENCE *laughs*.

A fireman.

LAURENCE. No way.

SARA. Yes.

LAURENCE. You're playing with me.

SARA. I'd never do that.

LAURENCE. I don't mind.

SARA. I'm a fireman. It's true. In the sense that I put out fires. Pretty appropriate in the circumstances.

LAURENCE. How's that?

SARA. In the case of this particular client, a consortium, they've built an oil pipeline right across the Sahara.

LAURENCE. The one you can see from space?

SARA. That's the one. They were fine until they got to the north of the country. Then some locals started blowing it up.

LAURENCE. Hence the fires.

SARA. Yes! A regular conflagration.

LAURENCE. And you put water on fires.

SARA. I help the consortium manage the situation.

3

LAURENCE. A consultant.

SARA. Of sorts. Specialise in clients with, how to put it…

LAURENCE. Image problems.

SARA. Deal with the media. Stop a few isolated incidents turning into a PR disaster back home. Help the client get their side of the story out.

LAURENCE. Their side?

SARA. The message.

LAURENCE. Pipelines are good.

SARA. There are a lot of misconceptions about pipelines. We offer a different narrative. Economic benefits. The schools the consortium builds. The hospitals it funds.

LAURENCE. Makes sense.

SARA. It's an art.

LAURENCE. I can see that. So you work with journalists?

SARA. Sometimes.

LAURENCE. You must have some stories.

SARA. One or two.

LAURENCE. Go on…

SARA. We buy them a few drinks, establish relations.

LAURENCE. You buy the drinks? I like that. They must love you.

SARA. Hacks hunt in packs, easy to chivvy along. With the requisite lightness of touch, of course.

She leans in.

Old soaks, the correspondents out here.

LAURENCE. Really?

SARA. The crowd doesn't change much. There are the adrenalin junkies, and the ones who don't go home because they've forgotten where it is. But the earnest ones are the worst. No sense of humour.

Pause.

4

LAURENCE. So you come out here often?

SARA (*drinks*). Wrong job for me, really, I hate flying. You've been to Lagos before?

LAURENCE. No.

SARA. You should come out some time. Lagos can be fun once you're safely installed in a hotel. Where are you staying?

LAURENCE. The Hilton.

SARA. Fantastic!

LAURENCE. So they say.

SARA. The Minister of Finance is having a grand bash at his villa on Ikoyi island next week. Pool party. No expense spared; ice sculptures peeing champagne the last time.

LAURENCE. Sounds good.

SARA. I can get you on the list.

LAURENCE. Fantastic!

SARA. I know.

LAURENCE. I won't be in Lagos that long.

SARA. That's a shame.

LAURENCE. It's only a stopover before I go up north.

SARA. Up north?

LAURENCE. Yeah.

SARA. How come you're going up north?

LAURENCE. I'm a journalist.

SARA *stops smiling*. LAURENCE *grins*.

Scene Two

Early morning. The corner of a hotel lobby in a northern Nigerian city, with the usual couple of easy chairs, couch and coffee table. CHUKS is asleep on the couch with a newspaper over his face.

CHUKS is wearing a shirt and suit trousers. The suit jacket is slung over the back of a chair.

A hotel PORTER comes in to the lobby, carrying a set of keys that jangle as he puts on the jacket of his bellboy-style uniform. The PORTER spots CHUKS and yanks the newspaper off his face.

PORTER. What do you think you are doing?

CHUKS. Excuse me?

PORTER. You cannot sleep there.

CHUKS. Why not?

PORTER. It is reserved for guests.

    CHUKS sits up, bleary.

CHUKS. What guests? Have they come from Lagos?

PORTER. I haven't even opened the door.

CHUKS. What time is it?

PORTER. Early.

    CHUKS lies back down.

    Hey, hey.

CHUKS. Hey what?

PORTER. It is not enough that you are hanging around here in the day? Now you are sleeping here?

CHUKS. Is this not a hotel?

PORTER. You want to sleep here, pay, go upstairs.

    The PORTER pokes CHUKS in the ribs. CHUKS gets off the couch, casts around for his jacket.

    You cannot be here. The manager will see you.

CHUKS. You locked me inside last night.

6

PORTER. Is that so? Where were you hiding?

CHUKS. I was here.

PORTER. In the toilet? In the kitchen?

CHUKS. You are blind.

PORTER. Don't vex me.

   CHUKS *puts on his jacket. It doesn't go with the trousers.*

   I will call the manager.

CHUKS. You won't do it.

PORTER. I am going to call him, oh…

CHUKS. You are still here.

   CHUKS *straightens his mismatched suit with a flourish.*

   The office is open.

PORTER. Your trouser no rhyme your shirt.

   There is a banging at the hotel entrance.

CHUKS. The door, eh?

   The PORTER *goes to open up.* CHUKS *sits hurriedly on a chair, picks up the discarded newspaper and pretends to read it.* DAVE *comes in to the hotel lobby carrying a travel bag and a laptop case. The* PORTER *follows.*

PORTER. Let me take that, sir.

   He takes DAVE*'s bag.*

   I will wake up the receptionist.

   The PORTER *leaves the lobby.* DAVE *sits on the couch. He flicks through a notebook.* CHUKS *watches* DAVE *for a while then moves over to sit next to him, a bit closer than is comfortable.* DAVE *looks up.*

CHUKS. Can I sit here?

DAVE. Sure.

   CHUKS *nods in the direction the* PORTER *went.*

CHUKS. If he brings the manager, say I am with you.

DAVE. But I'm not with you.

CHUKS. Now we are talking, we are together.

DAVE. Is there a problem?

CHUKS. You want to know?

DAVE. It might be wise.

CHUKS. If I am not with you, I must dash the manager some naira to sit here.

DAVE. I see. Why don't you book a room?

CHUKS (*laughs*). The presidential suite is not available.

DAVE *goes back to his notebook.*

You are a journalist.

DAVE. How can you tell?

CHUKS *nods at the laptop.*

Oh. Yes.

CHUKS. You don't travel up to the north often.

DAVE. Not if I can help it. I'm here for the fire.

CHUKS. On the pipeline. Of course.

DAVE. You know about that?

CHUKS. Yes.

DAVE. What do you know about it?

CHUKS. I know many things. It is my business.

DAVE. You're a fixer?

CHUKS (*grins*). Independent facilitator extraordinaire. Let me show you my portfolio.

CHUKS *rummages in a pocket and produces a small wadge of snapshots. He hands one to* DAVE.

DAVE. What's this?

CHUKS. Polio.

DAVE. What?

CHUKS. I know this one girl. Five years old, has polio.

DAVE. Sorry to hear that.

CHUKS. You know what happened to her?

DAVE. I'm sure it's sad.

CHUKS. Her legs, they bended.

    CHUKS *mimes a slow bending action with both arms*.

    The legs don' bend make K. Now everybody calls her K-leg.

DAVE. About the pipeline fire…

CHUKS. Her mother is always shouting at her.

    CHUKS *mimics a woman's voice*.

    'K-leg, K-leg. Come here, K-leg, shut up, K-leg.'

DAVE. Why are you showing me this?

CHUKS. Would you like to do an interview with her?

DAVE. No.

CHUKS. The price is very reasonable. One hour, one hundred dollars US.

    DAVE *hands the picture back*.

DAVE. About the fire…

CHUKS. You can speak to the mother, take your own snaps. The girl cannot speak English, but I can interpret.

DAVE. Can you.

CHUKS. For a small-small commission. I was teaching English before, three years in a secondary school. Translation, interviewees, transportation arranged. I can be your window to understanding this country.

DAVE. I've been here years. I get it perfectly well.

    CHUKS *snorts*.

CHUKS. I can tell you what the people are really thinking.

DAVE. Look, I'm only interested in what's going on with the pipeline fire.

CHUKS. But polio is a good story.

DAVE. The fire.

CHUKS. Fire, fire. All of your colleagues, they will be writing about the fire.

DAVE. That's sort of the point.

CHUKS. Allow me to finish my presentation. We are both professionals here.

DAVE. All right, all right.

CHUKS *hands over another snap.*

CHUKS. Thank you. Now, this woman, they beat her when the *maitatsine* were rioting last year. I found her, brought the journalist to her. He said it was a productive and fruitful interview.

DAVE *studies the photo.*

They put her picture in the *New York Times*.

DAVE. Think I remember that. How much?

CHUKS. Round trip to Kaduna, hourly rate plus translation services and naira to dash the husband. Three hundred US, package.

CHUKS *flips out another picture.*

This is the same riots.

DAVE *laughs suddenly when he sees it.*

DAVE. Christ.

CHUKS. They were playing football with the head.

CHUKS *offers the next photo.*

This is the best, look at this.

DAVE *takes it and whistles.*

I took a client to see this one after the election troubles.

DAVE. What happened to him?

CHUKS. Battery acid.

DAVE *holds the picture up to the light, turning it to find the best angle.*

There is not much news in the north, but when something happens, it is good. You people come here looking for violence and bad things. I can get it for you, I am very reliable.

DAVE. So you'll help me with the fire.

CHUKS. *Kai!*

DAVE. I want to know about the boys.

CHUKS. The fire is nothing. (*Indicates his photos.*) I came here to talk about this.

DAVE. Do you know about the boys? You must know something. You said you were a professional.

Pause.

CHUKS. Okay, okay. The fire.

DAVE. Thank fuck. At last.

CHUKS. You see, essentially what we have in this situation is some vigilante boys with big mouths making trouble.

DAVE. And?

CHUKS. They are saying the pipeline is a vacuum, it will suck the oil from the country, take the wealth away.

DAVE. And?

CHUKS. So the western companies, they built the pipeline near to here, now the boys are exploding it.

DAVE. Are they serious?

CHUKS. Very serious. Very serious. No smoke without fire.

DAVE. Armed?

CHUKS. AKs.

DAVE. Do you know how to find them?

CHUKS. No.

DAVE. You must have some idea.

CHUKS. No.

DAVE. I can make it worth your while.

CHUKS. You are not listening to me.

The PORTER *returns with* DAVE*'s bag and drops it at his feet.*

PORTER. The hotel is full.

DAVE. What?

PORTER. The hotel is full, sir.

DAVE. Since when? I booked. I phoned from Lagos.

PORTER. The receptionist, he says the hotel is full.

DAVE. What palaver now? He wants me to find him something, is that it? Him chop, you chop, eh? (*To* CHUKS.) Okay. Let's talk more about this. I'll buy you a beer. Don't move, I'll be right back, we can work this out then.

DAVE *turns briefly on his way out.*

Sorry, I didn't catch your name.

CHUKS. Chuks.

DAVE. I'm Dave. Well, Chuks, you've some nasty pictures.

CHUKS. It's business.

DAVE *goes.*

PORTER. He wants you to take him to the boys?

CHUKS. You did not bring the manager. I knew it!

PORTER. He was sleeping.

CHUKS. You were afraid to awake him.

PORTER. You are taking that journalist to the boys?

CHUKS *shrugs.*

CHUKS. I take him, I don't take him, na what?

PORTER. You no dey fear? After the last time? Those boys who dey paint their face, wear invisibility amulet, they say bullet no go touch them. Today they set fire here, tomorrow, three hundred kilometre there. I heard that they appear, disappear like magic.

CHUKS. Who told you that? They are not invisible. If today they are here… (*Indicates one point.*) and tomorrow they reach there…

He indicates another spot. The PORTER *leans in, rapt.*

… then that is because they have a car.

The PORTER *sucks his teeth and walks off.*

Wait. You have a beer delivery?

The PORTER *stops.*

PORTER. Gulder.

CHUKS. Is that the only one you have?

PORTER. No Star this time.

CHUKS. Guinness?

The PORTER *hesitates.*

There is.

PORTER. Stock is low. There are only two crates remaining.

CHUKS. Bring one.

The PORTER *doesn't move.*

For me, eh? You know my face.

The PORTER *goes out.* CHUKS *takes out a mobile phone and checks it, then checks second and third phones too. The* PORTER *returns with a crate of beer.*

Wonderful.

He hands some money to the PORTER, *who counts it.*

PORTER. Do better.

CHUKS. Impossible.

PORTER. This is wholesale price.

CHUKS. *Kai!* You go bankrupt me, my friend.

CHUKS *hands some more cash over.*

That is what I can afford. More than last time, less than next time.

After a moment, the PORTER *pockets the cash.* CHUKS *sits back down.*

PORTER. So, take it go.

CHUKS. Later.

PORTER. The manager will see it.

CHUKS. Later, my friend.

PORTER. *Abeg*, you go put me for trouble. He said he may promote me. To barman.

CHUKS. Why?

PORTER. I took his car for him, helped him queue for petrol.

CHUKS. You queued for him?

PORTER. Two days.

CHUKS *snorts*.

CHUKS. Okay, remove it to the corner.

He indicates a not-too-obvious spot for the crate. The PORTER *is still troubled*.

What you dey fear, eh? The manager is sleeping. Everything dey fear you.

Pause.

He will not promote you. He just wants you to queue for him. He will tell you 'next time, next time'. Open your eyes, help yourself if you don't want to suffer in this life. Things they were bad in the south, so I came to the north. When I was a teacher they did not pay my salary for many months. You know what I was doing during that time? I started selling *moimoi* and *akara* to the students. But it didn't taste good, I cannot cook. I had no money for pocket. So I started importing bushmeat from Jos.

PORTER. Bushmeat?

CHUKS. Grasscutter. I had to stop because my house was smelling.

PORTER. *Kai!*

CHUKS. From there, I was selling the end-of-year English examination paper to the students, their parents. Before the examination.

PORTER. Is that good business?

CHUKS. Until they sacked me.

PORTER. And you are telling me don't fear?

CHUKS *taps the beer crate*.

CHUKS. You know what is this? Local-brewed Guinness. Stronger. Eight per cent. They are smuggling it back to Ireland now, those people don't want to drink their own water brew. Don't fear. They can sell Guinness to Ireland. Anything you can see, somebody will buy it. Is suffering not a commodity? Bad news? Pack am, sell am.

CHUKS *moves the crate to the spot he indicated earlier.* JEROME, *a dapper American, enters from reception, walking stiffly.* CHUKS *freezes.*

PORTER. Good morning, sir.

JEROME *just stares at* CHUKS. *The* PORTER *makes himself scarce.*

CHUKS. *Sannu.*

JEROME. *Yauwa, sannu.*

There is an awkward moment.

CHUKS. I am going, eh. I am only…

CHUKS *collects himself. He goes to shake* JEROME*'s hand.*

Jerome. Long time no see.

JEROME. Yeah.

CHUKS. How are things?

JEROME. Things are great.

CHUKS. I am very happy to hear that.

JEROME. Still fixing?

CHUKS. Now and then, now and then.

JEROME. How's business?

CHUKS. It is good. Very good. I opened a bar now also.

JEROME. You did?

CHUKS. Madam Hannah.

JEROME. Catchy.

CHUKS. I called it for my daughter. It is near the edge of town. It is not like the fancy one here, only one small room but the, what is it, ambience is very nice. You should come there.

JEROME. Yeah, maybe.

CHUKS. I just bought a new fridge.

JEROME. A fridge.

CHUKS. Imported.

> CHUKS *counts out the fridge's functions on his fingers.*

> With ice-maker, freezer compartment, automatic defrost mode…

> CHUKS *tails off.*

> Why are you coming to this place again? Are you looking for a story?

JEROME. Not this time.

CHUKS. I don't believe you.

JEROME. I'm not a journalist any more.

CHUKS. Then why are you here?

JEROME. I'm working for the pipeline consortium.

CHUKS. Eh?

JEROME. Took a job there. Press Officer. Corporate communications.

CHUKS. Are you joking?

JEROME. No.

CHUKS. Because *joke na joke*…

> JEROME *is serious.*

> Congratulations.

JEROME. Thanks.

CHUKS. *Kai!* Well, this is a good thing, eh? Journalism is a terrible profession. Very hard work, always looking for trouble. Too much up and down, up and down, running around.

> JEROME *sits, gingerly.* CHUKS *notes this.*

> So you are a big man now.

JEROME. I wouldn't say that.

CHUKS. Come on. This is me you are talking to. That is a nice suit. They gave you a good deal, am I correct?

JEROME. Can't complain.

CHUKS (*laughs*). Well done. Jerome.

JEROME. So look, I'm up here to talk to some people from the consortium's northern office. Your friends finally blew up the pipeline.

CHUKS. How are they my friends?

JEROME. They didn't shoot *you*.

CHUKS (*raises hands in surrender*). Sorry about that. I did not know when I took you that the boys would do that. It is the foreigners they don't like.

Pause.

Anyway, you look very well.

JEROME. Yeah.

CHUKS. Hale and hearty. A bit fattier than before. The leg is okay?

JEROME. My ass is fine. Thanks for asking.

Pause.

CHUKS. You are the one that wanted to go there.

JEROME. True.

Pause.

This new fire on the pipeline; the place is going to be crawling with reporters soon.

CHUKS. Is that so?

JEROME. Looking for someone like you to help them find the boys, probably.

CHUKS. After what happened to you? They no fear?

JEROME. Won't make any difference.

CHUKS. No way. The boys are bringing *wahala* around here. Stirring up trouble. I told you they were serious. I don't deal with them any more.

JEROME. So what are you doing here?

CHUKS. I have diversified. I came to offer them a story about polio.

JEROME. Polio? Are you fucking serious? Polio came and went.

CHUKS. It is still here.

JEROME. Let me explain something to you. You don't get to decide what the news is. Today, the news is the boys torched the pipeline. I think you should leave before you end up doing something you don't want to. We're both lucky to be alive. They warned you.

CHUKS. I am not taking anybody to the boys. You think me I am stupid?

JEROME. You'd pass up an opportunity?

CHUKS. Yes.

JEROME. I'm glad to hear that. The consortium would obviously prefer it that way.

CHUKS. If the journalists want to go to the boys, they can follow the smoke.

JEROME. I really think it would be better if you didn't take any more reporters down there to see them.

CHUKS. No, no.

JEROME. To be sure, I'll make it worth your while. Go look after your bar for a couple days; this thing'll blow over.

JEROME *pulls out his wallet and extracts some cash.*

Here, how's this, let's see…

CHUKS. No, no, no. Forget that. Come on, my friend, put it away. For you there is no obligation.

JEROME. So how do I know you won't take them?

CHUKS. There is no need. Last year was last year.

CHUKS *passes a card to* JEROME.

You see. Here is my card.

JEROME. 'Madam Hannah.'

CHUKS. Right now business is booming. Before, when you saw me, I was eating zero zero one, you know?

JEROME. Zero zero one?

CHUKS. No breakfast, no lunch. Only dinner.

JEROME. What can you do, huh?

CHUKS. I had to adjust my stomach. It is different now.

> CHUKS *slaps* JEROME *on the back.*

> Anyway, I am going. I am going now. Welcome to the north again, it is very nice to see you. You are looking well. Very healthy.

JEROME. Bye.

> CHUKS *walks a few steps before remembering something. He turns back.*

CHUKS. Ah. Sorry. Can I collect it?

> CHUKS *indicates the card in* JEROME's *hand.* JEROME *hands it back.* CHUKS *salutes before heading rapidly out of the lobby.*

JEROME. Christ.

> *He spots the beer crate that* CHUKS *has forgotten in the corner and drags himself over to it. After a brief investigation,* JEROME *takes a beer and returns to his seat. He cracks the bottle open and drinks.*

Scene Three

Late morning. DAVE *searches the lobby for* CHUKS. JEROME *enters. They shake hands warmly.*

JEROME. Dave. Expected you sooner.

DAVE. You got up here fast.

JEROME. Last night. Things to smooth out.

DAVE. What's the inside info?

JEROME. On the fire? Officially? An isolated incident.

DAVE. And unofficially?

JEROME. An isolated incident.

DAVE. That's not what you'd have said before.

JEROME. I work for the consortium now.

DAVE. How's the dark side treating you?

JEROME. Pays better.

DAVE *looks round again*.

DAVE. Did you see a man?

JEROME. What man?

DAVE. In a bad suit. A cheap suit. All over me like a cheap suit. Chuks, I think.

JEROME. No.

DAVE. I've been looking for him for an hour now. He's a fixer.

JEROME. No shit.

DAVE. He was waiting for me. You might have seen him.

JEROME. No, Dave, I haven't seen anybody.

SARA *and* LAURENCE *enter, both with luggage*.

LAURENCE. I'd like a briefing.

SARA. What?

LAURENCE. A briefing. That's what you do, right? I'd like you to explain what's going on up here.

SARA. Jerome will be briefing later. He's the Regional Head of Communications. I'm sure he'd be more than happy to do a sit-down to explain why the pipeline is essential to the future prosperity of the north and its people. Look, he's...

LAURENCE. I'd like to talk to you.

SARA *hands* LAURENCE *a business card*.

SARA. Let's talk when you're settled in.

LAURENCE. Doesn't it bother you?

SARA. What?

LAURENCE. Being a mouthpiece. You know what the consortium does, don't you? Moves in, starts siphoning the oil away. Not for the locals' benefit, all for its own interests. They've made a mess down south.

SARA. This situation isn't linked to the south, but lessons have been learned.

20

LAURENCE. I mean, how long have these guys been in the country? Years? Decades now? Where'd all the money go? You see things getting better for anyone in that time?

SARA. That's a governmental issue. It's not…

LAURENCE. Except the Minister of Finance, of course. I'm sure he's doing all right. When's the pool party again? Should I buy a sarong?

SARA. Would you let me finish? Don't you think some of the responsibility lies here?

LAURENCE. No wonder the locals are angry with greedy polluters building pipelines. Transporting oil across their land. I'm going to get their story out, the truth. And the truth is going to be shit-poor people and blackening soil and stinking dead-fish rivers. Not in your narrative, is it?

SARA *walks away, toward* DAVE *and* JEROME.

Hope I'm not being too earnest.

LAURENCE *takes his backpack to check in*.

DAVE. Hi, Sara.

SARA. Hello, Dave. Jerome.

JEROME *nods*.

(*To* DAVE.) I guessed you might turn up. Thought I saw you get on the plane, but I wasn't sure.

DAVE. First on. Back row.

SARA. I hate these internal flights.

DAVE. Reconditioned.

SARA. What?

DAVE. That plane. Creaky. Last time I flew in one of those, a door burst open and the stewardess had to wrestle it shut in mid-air. Lucky it was low altitude, so it didn't depressurise. Higher up and…

SARA. That's impossible.

DAVE. You'd think.

SARA. Sorry to hear you're leaving us.

DAVE. What?

SARA. Going home. Your paper's cutting back on Africa or something?

DAVE. Who told you that?

SARA. Someone said, I think. I can't remember exactly. I probably misheard.

DAVE. I'm not leaving.

SARA. No?

DAVE. I like it here. I like it here a lot.

SARA. I totally agree. Lagos isn't so bad. I mean, there are better oil postings. Aleppo's nice. But Baku, after Baku, Lagos is great...

DAVE. Well, yes. Look, I'll leave you two to it.

DAVE *goes out.*

SARA. Jerome, you should view me being here as an extra resource. A spare pair of...

JEROME *jerks his hands up.*

JEROME. Two's fine.

SARA. Look, I'm not so keen to step on your toes that I'd willingly get on some second-hand aircraft with seventies wallpaper and made-in-Taiwan spare parts.

JEROME. You should have had them lay on a car.

SARA. No official car journeys over twenty kilometres. Company policy. It's the carjackings.

JEROME. You didn't need to come up here. It's under control.

SARA. I'll handle external calls, you take care of the reporters.

JEROME. I can do both. You just kick back and relax. There's a nice pool out back.

SARA. The consortium would prefer it if I handle external calls, and you take care of the reporters. That arrangement makes sense, you used to be one of that lot, you know how they operate.

JEROME. There's also a mini-golf course. Cute. Except somebody took a dump right by the mini-windmill. That's not so good, but…

SARA. I'll handle external calls, you take care of the reporters.

JEROME. Fine.

SARA. You've set up the briefing?

JEROME. It's at three.

She sits with him.

SARA. Do they do anything except beer?

JEROME. I don't think so, Sara.

SARA. Gin and tonic?

JEROME. Probably not.

SARA. I'd quite like a gin and tonic. Actually, I could murder one. You'd think gin and tonic would be more popular round here. Quinine for the mozzies. Are those two the only journos that have come up from Lagos?

JEROME. So far. Maybe the Associated Press stringer later.

SARA. It's a manageable number. With any luck they'll stick around the hotel.

JEROME. Don't be too sure.

SARA. What makes you think that?

JEROME. Dave's a smart guy, he'll find his way out to where the action is.

SARA. Can't you persuade him it's not worth it?

JEROME. How would I do that?

SARA. He's your friend.

JEROME. Sara, you can't just parachute in here. I was promised autonomy in this role.

SARA. And I completely respect your autonomy, Jerome. But you know we're also part of something bigger. Just pretend I'm not here.

JEROME. Excuse me?

SARA. I'd better check in. Wonder where the porter is.

SARA picks up her suitcase and leaves. JEROME drinks a while. DAVE returns, with LAURENCE in hot pursuit. JEROME observes with amusement.

LAURENCE. Want a beer?

DAVE. I was just...

LAURENCE. We should talk. Good to see a familiar face up here.

DAVE. Who did you say you worked for again?

LAURENCE. Paying my own way. Got a contact on the *Daily Post* newsdesk, I'm hoping they'll take something.

DAVE. You'll be lucky.

LAURENCE. I told them my father's from this part of the world, there's a connection. Actually, it's not as easy as I thought, getting around.

Pause.

I have a question. If you know where the best place is to find a fixer.

DAVE. A fixer?

LAURENCE. Someone useful on the ground.

DAVE. Yes, I know what a fixer is. Something you had in mind?

LAURENCE. I'm going to find the boys. Better than reporting from a hotel room.

DAVE. Not a smart idea to go out looking for those thugs. They're an unfriendly bunch. Nasty pieces of work.

LAURENCE. That's just the consortium line. I think they're entitled to be angry, they should be angry.

DAVE. Good luck with it.

DAVE edges away, but LAURENCE persists.

LAURENCE. There's got to be somebody up here who knows someone.

DAVE. Anything's possible. You could try the airport hotel, that sort often hangs around there.

LAURENCE. Where's that?

DAVE. Near the airport.

Pause.

LAURENCE. Thanks.

DAVE. If you get a whiff of one, let me know.

LAURENCE. Of course.

Pause.

You know what, I just want to say how much I admire your work, Dave. I think it's great.

DAVE *makes a modest noise.*

No, no, really. Like that Burkina Faso series.

DAVE. That was a while ago.

LAURENCE. And that feature where you were barbecuing crabs with rebels on a mined beach in… in… Eritrea.

DAVE. Somalia.

LAURENCE. Dangerman Dave. You should make that your byline.

DAVE. Yeah, maybe. Look, why don't you get that round, eh?

LAURENCE, *delighted, goes to get the beers.* DAVE *sits with* JEROME.

JEROME. Your new friend's kind of sweet.

DAVE. Sweet like bloody toothache.

JEROME. Trying to lose him?

DAVE. *Inshallah.* How's your leg?

JEROME. Peachy, Dave.

DAVE. They got the bullet out yet?

JEROME. It's still in there.

DAVE. Must be a pain at airport security, eh?

JEROME. What?

DAVE. Setting off metal detectors.

JEROME. Not really.

DAVE. Jerome, I need to get out there. Pronto. Track down the boys.

JEROME. It's not wise.

DAVE. I'll take my chances. I'm grown up, remember?

JEROME. Dangerman.

DAVE. I need a fixer, someone who knows the terrain.

JEROME. Not sure I can help.

DAVE. The man I found earlier…

JEROME. Lost him?

DAVE. Come on. Someone must have taken you down there on that non-story last year. Back when you were still on the side of the angels.

JEROME. Dave…

DAVE. Was it him? The guy I met earlier. It was him, right? Chuks?

JEROME. I'm out of the game now.

DAVE. You'll be back in the fold. Too much fun to quit. Roast crab on the beach, remember? Somalia.

JEROME. Too long.

DAVE. We've poured a libation in every misery hole this side of the Sahara.

DAVE *tips some of* JEROME*'s beer on the floor.*

See, and one here.

JEROME (*laughs*). It's been good.

DAVE. Give me a name. Nothing that will cause you trouble, just a name.

JEROME. Dave…

DAVE. I need something good. Haven't had anything in the paper for a while. They'll cut me loose. You heard.

JEROME. No they won't.

DAVE. You got out at the right time, I tell you. No call for Africa stories at the moment. Space is tight. Every time I call the desk it's the same thing. 'Space is tight.' You know what I have to do to get anything in these days?

JEROME. Say please?

DAVE. Very funny. No, there's interest in the pipeline. Genuine honest-to-God interest. The desk called me, can you imagine? They haven't called me in months. I've got to get something good on this or I tell you they'll cut me loose for sure.

JEROME. What would you do?

DAVE. I'd have to go home.

JEROME. Shit.

DAVE. I can't face it, Jerome. Can't face it. I went back last year, to see my mother.

JEROME. Where is she now?

DAVE. Bournemouth. It's by the seaside. It was exactly like death. Like going from colour TV to black-and-white. I couldn't stand it. Didn't know what to do with myself, you know?

JEROME. Yeah. I know. But you're putting me in a difficult position.

DAVE. They're all flying out now, these kids, looking for a pipeline story. That sanctimonious tit you just saw, he came up to me in Lagos last week. Said, 'Hey, how are you doing, can you give me some contacts...' (*Drops his voice.*) Come on, something for me?

JEROME. I'm sorry. I...

DAVE. How's your boss?

JEROME. She's not my boss.

DAVE. Right.

JEROME. She's a consultant. You know that.

DAVE. Seems to enjoy her little trips.

JEROME. Out to Lagos, yes. I'm sure she doesn't want to be up here.

DAVE. Really? You sure? 'Cause I reckon she really, really wants to be here. I mean, she hates internal flights.

JEROME. She didn't want to come.

DAVE. Shows how far she'll go to fuck you over. When did you last see her out of the compound? Never leaves, even though it's a clusterfuck in there. Single girl, the wives think she's after their husbands. Can't blame them, Landesman's had his eye on her.

JEROME. Really? Landesman?

DAVE. Yes.

JEROME. I'll be fucked. You?

DAVE. Wouldn't say no.

JEROME. Please tell me not.

DAVE. You know how it is. She's standing in Piccadilly Circus, four out of ten, stick her down in the Lagos compound, she's suddenly a nine point five, if you catch my drift.

JEROME *laughs*.

You living in there now?

JEROME. Yeah. The place came with the job. Plenty of square feet.

DAVE. Bit corporate, those apartments.

JEROME. You trying to get at something?

DAVE. Just teasing. No, I respect your decision. It was the right time to get out of journalism. Absolutely the right time. Wish I had.

Pause.

Still, wouldn't want your gig, explaining the consortium. Knowing what that lot have been up to down in the south.

JEROME. This isn't the delta.

DAVE. Not pretty, Jerome, though, is it? You used to say that yourself. Back when you used to stick it to the man.

JEROME. And now I'm the man?

DAVE. Course not, Jerome, course not.

JEROME. Fuck you, Dave.

Pause.

I shouldn't do this.

DAVE. Yes, you should.

JEROME. That guy Chuks. Runs a bar not too far away.

DAVE. Where?

JEROME. Edge of the city.

DAVE. I'd be grateful.

JEROME. You didn't get it from me.

JEROME *produces a notebook and scribbles something down for* DAVE. DAVE *takes it and stands.*

DAVE. Thanks. I'll remember this.

JEROME. What, heading out now?

DAVE. See you later.

JEROME. You owe me.

DAVE *hurries out.* LAURENCE *returns with the beers, looks around for* DAVE.

He left.

LAURENCE. You're Jerome. I didn't realise. Got a moment?

JEROME *indicates the next seat.*

You used to be a reporter.

JEROME. True.

LAURENCE. Why'd you quit?

JEROME. It got boring.

LAURENCE. You going to help me out?

JEROME. No, kid.

LAURENCE. Thought everyone pulled together out here.

JEROME. Up to a point.

LAURENCE *notices the* PORTER *come in. The* PORTER *has taken off his uniform jacket, which is slung over his shoulder. As he walks past, he notices with irritation that the beer crate is still there and picks it up.* LAURENCE *gets up and pursues the* PORTER *out of the lobby.*

Scene Four

A small bar.

Not much more than a couple of rickety melamine-topped tables and a few stools. To one side is a large, dominating fridge-freezer.

CHUKS *is cleaning tables. The* PORTER *comes in, carrying the beer crate from the hotel. He thumps it down on the floor.*

PORTER. I worked in the night. I am tired. Instead of going to my room to sleep, I trekked across town with your crate. You left it there the whole time. You want me to lose my job?

CHUKS. Sorry, I forgot to take it.

PORTER. No bus. No taxi. No nothing, nobody in the road. People don' run home, dey fear trouble. I heard that the army is coming to crack down on the boys. It was on the radio. They say they will bring the curfew again if the army comes here. Even the women dey fry *akara* on the street they don' pack, go.

The PORTER *looks round the bar.*

Why did you run back here?

CHUKS. To open.

PORTER. Nobody is here.

CHUKS. People are staying in their house.

PORTER. Last time I came here, nobody was here.

CHUKS. It is one p.m. Who is drinking at one p.m?

PORTER. Did you not see them in the hotel? Immediately they came there them dey drink beer the same like water. *Kai!* It was busy. Not like here.

CHUKS. Business is booming.

PORTER. You ran back for this?

CHUKS. I don' tire.

PORTER. Come on. I saw you. That journalist that they shot his backside, he was talking to you.

CHUKS. He is no longer a journalist.

PORTER. You ran away.

CHUKS. Who knew he would come back?

PORTER. And you are telling me 'don't fear don't fear'.

CHUKS. Just bring it.

The PORTER *moves the crate closer.* CHUKS *looks it over.*

One is missing. Did you take it?

PORTER. Of course not!

Pause.

I don't know why I even brought this for you, I was the only person in the road, carrying your thing. We are finished in business, you hear? No more deals. Stop hanging around.

CHUKS. No problem.

PORTER. The manager he is going to interview me tomorrow for barman. If I get the job, no more wheeler-dealer *wahala* with you.

CHUKS. Okay. See how far you will get.

Pause.

PORTER. What about the pressmen that came today for the fire?

CHUKS. I don't care.

PORTER. What?

CHUKS. This pipeline business is not good. I am not coming back to the hotel.

PORTER. Okay.

CHUKS. When you left there, what were they doing?

PORTER. You said you don't care.

Pause.

They are looking for cars.

CHUKS. They are going to the pipeline? Somebody is taking them?

PORTER. I don't know. They asked one taxi to carry them, the driver said no. So instead they interviewed him. And also me. One of them asked me what did I think about the pipeline.

CHUKS. He asked *you*?

PORTER (*emphasising unfamiliar term*). Vox pop.

The PORTER *laughs.*

I said they build pipeline they don't build it, either way what is the difference? It is still monkey dey work, baboon dey chop in this country. The thing I don't understand is, why do they want to go there? The boys will show them pepper.

CHUKS. That is what they are looking for.

PORTER. This one journalist, he came to me. He was looking for you.

CHUKS. For me? Which one?

PORTER. The small small boy. He said his father is from here. He said he heard about one man they call Chuks, did I know this Chuks. I said, 'Of course, sir, I know Chuks. Everybody knows Chuks!'

CHUKS. And you said what?

PORTER. I said, 'Chuks he don' go to his bar.' He asked the road and I told him. Maybe he will come.

CHUKS. To here?

PORTER. You see, I can do your kind of business. I don' clinch the deal for you.

CHUKS *sucks his teeth.*

What is doing you?

CHUKS. I am not doing business today. I went there, I told them what is the thing they should write, polio. They don't want to write it. They want *wahala*, end of story. And you are telling them to come here.

PORTER. Sorry, eh?

Pause.

What are you going to do?

CHUKS. I do not know.

PORTER. No problem. You will think of something. You are very intelligent.

Pause.

CHUKS. Go and sleep.

PORTER. Okay.

The PORTER *doesn't move.*

CHUKS. Oh.

He indicates the beer.

Take one go. Two.

The PORTER *helps himself. But he doesn't leave, and sits down instead.*

PORTER. If I get the barman job, we will be competitors. Although my clientele will be different from yours.

CHUKS. How will we be competitors? You would be a barman…

PORTER. Yes.

CHUKS. Barman. I am a bar owner. This is *my* bar.

PORTER. What is doing you?

Scene Five

The bar. DAVE *stands by one of the tables. He's wearing a utility jacket with lots of pockets, and a hefty satellite phone with its big antenna is on the table.* CHUKS *is close by.*

DAVE. I'm on a deadline. I've got to press you on this.

CHUKS. I can't help you.

DAVE. I need to find the boys. Got to get this interview in the bag.

CHUKS. The boys are bad men.

DAVE. That's what we like. Militants in balaclavas. Serious demands.

CHUKS. You are playing with fire.

DAVE. You're the fixer, right? So fix it. You've got contacts.

CHUKS. Every day every day you people come. Some problems,
I can help. Some things – the boys – no, I cannot. I don't
know where they are.

DAVE. This morning you said...

CHUKS. This morning was this morning.

DAVE. Before you ran off, those things you showed me.

CHUKS. Yes.

DAVE. They were good pictures, Chuks. Sharp copy. Especially
that little moppet. Sad story, big brown eyes. Family didn't care.

CHUKS. That is somebody's daughter you are talking about.

DAVE. Ah. Sorry, didn't mean to imply... you know. Look, the
point is, you're the man to speak to in a pinch.

CHUKS. Because why?

DAVE. Good man, I heard. Reliable, knows anyone worth
knowing. Now I'm in that pinch.

CHUKS. I don't know the boys. I don't know where to find them.
I don't have anything to do with such people.

DAVE. You took Jerome to see them last year.

CHUKS. Look at what happened to him.

DAVE. I see. You're a smart man. You're looking for a little
negotiation. Okay, I can do that.

 DAVE *produces a wadge of naira notes, peels off a few and
slaps them down on the table.* CHUKS *stares at the money.*

Ten thousand. Good start? Sorry, I've only got naira on me.
Should have brought dollars.

 CHUKS *is agitated.* DAVE *watches him closely, puts some
more cash down.*

Twenty thousand.

CHUKS. I have already told you.

DAVE. What?

CHUKS. Where the boys are hiding, I don't know. Maybe in the bush, maybe in the lake swimming with *mammy water*.

DAVE. Okay. I understand how this goes. I'm an old Africa hand.

CHUKS. You understand?

DAVE. I'll put some more zeros on the table. Thirty thousand.

DAVE *counts the money out.*

CHUKS. You are not hearing me. Ask around in the market.

DAVE. Tried there.

CHUKS. Then go somewhere else, another town, ask there. Kaduna.

DAVE. I heard the boys were based closer to here. The pipeline route.

CHUKS. Them dey call you? Then go yourself into the bush and find them.

DAVE. All right. You're good. I give up. Name your price.

CHUKS. What?

DAVE. Name it.

CHUKS (*plucks a figure from the air*). One hundred thousand.

DAVE. Done.

DAVE *retrieves more notes. He offers them to* CHUKS.

Should be about right.

CHUKS *stares at the large sum.*

You can sort it, then?

CHUKS *looks up slowly.* DAVE *slaps him heartily on the back.*

Good man, good man. Now, as you know, I'm on a bit of a schedule…

DAVE *stops short as* LAURENCE *comes through the door.* CHUKS *rapidly stuffs the cash from the table into a trouser pocket.* LAURENCE *grins at* DAVE, *and bounds over.*

LAURENCE. Dave!

DAVE. Laurence. What are you doing here?

LAURENCE. Same as you, I would guess, Dave. Chasing shady men down?

DAVE. Something like that.

LAURENCE. Seems you beat me to the fixer.

LAURENCE *extends a hand to* CHUKS.

Hey, how are you doing? Chukwuma, is it?

CHUKS. Chuks.

LAURENCE. Pleased to meet you. I've heard good things. Too bad Dangerman Dave got here first, or we might have been working together.

DAVE. Yeah, too bad.

LAURENCE. Well, seeing as I'm here anyway, I'll buy you guys a cold beer before I head back to the hotel.

DAVE. Thanks, Laurence. But it's a little early for me.

LAURENCE. Never.

DAVE *examines his watch and shoots a glance at* CHUKS.

DAVE. Not sure we have time.

LAURENCE. Nonsense. There's plenty. (*Pointing at the large fridge.*) Are they in there?

CHUKS *nods and goes to fetch some beers from the fridge.* LAURENCE *sits at a table, and* DAVE *eventually follows suit.*

(*Looking around.*) It's not the Lagos Hilton, but it's got atmosphere.

Pause.

What time did you leave then?

DAVE. Soon as I heard about the fixer.

LAURENCE. Who told you about him?

DAVE. The Associated Press stringer. You?

LAURENCE. I worked it out. Found a taxi in the end. Looks like you drive faster, though.

DAVE. Guess so.

LAURENCE. Terrible roads, Dave. Potholes like moon craters.

DAVE. Deeper.

LAURENCE. A few militants hiding out in those, for sure.

DAVE. Did you try looking inside?

LAURENCE. Funny, Dave. That's hilarious. No, thought I'd try here for the guided tour instead. As I say, too bad you beat me to it.

CHUKS brings the beers over with some glasses.
LAURENCE raises a toast.

Cheers. Good luck with the interview, Dangerman. Don't let the boys string you along.

Pause.

Or up.

DAVE*'s satellite phone starts to ring.*

You guys get satphones?

DAVE. Yes.

LAURENCE. That's great. I wasn't allowed to borrow one.

DAVE. Too bad.

LAURENCE. Budget cutbacks.

The phone is still ringing, but DAVE *is reluctant to answer it.*

Probably your newsdesk.

DAVE. Yes.

LAURENCE. Nice to be plugged in.

DAVE. Yes.

LAURENCE. Might be important.

LAURENCE answers the phone.

Hello?

DAVE *snatches the phone off* LAURENCE.

DAVE (*into phone*). Yes… Never mind… No, I told you I filed some pars on that one already. Shit. Hang on.

DAVE *looks at* LAURENCE *and* CHUKS. *Then he steps outside.*

LAURENCE. Prick.

CHUKS *takes a swig from his beer.*

My man. Nice place you have here.

CHUKS. Thank you.

LAURENCE. Good doing business with him?

CHUKS. Fine.

LAURENCE. What did he offer you? A few hundred?

CHUKS. That concerns him and myself.

LAURENCE. Can I say something?

CHUKS. Me, I don't want to...

LAURENCE. I want to get the local people's story out. I'm on your side, you understand.

CHUKS. Look, I...

LAURENCE (*cuts in*). Dave, his paper sides with foreign interests. He's going to go along with you, meet the boys, then do a big number on evil militants attacking the trans-Saharan pipeline, destroying the lawful property of a western consortium that has every legal right to be going about its business here.

CHUKS. But the boys are trouble.

LAURENCE. And that's the story he's going to write.

CHUKS. So what is the problem?

LAURENCE. I think the boys are misunderstood. He's going to misrepresent them. But I'm after the truth. The boys are right to believe pipeline-builders don't have your interests at heart. They come here to exploit. They don't care about you.

CHUKS. Look, I am not a politician. You can't change how this is. I don't care what the boys are thinking.

LAURENCE. Then you should do. You should want them to get their message out. You help me, and I can help them do that. Give Africa a voice.

CHUKS. What is the point of...

LAURENCE (*cuts in*). I am passionate about this.

CHUKS. They don't like me, and they don't trust foreigners and pressmen. Last year, that American journalist came up here and the boys shot him. In the buttock.

LAURENCE. So all you have to persuade them to do is make a slight alteration to their media strategy.

CHUKS. Come on, my friend.

LAURENCE. Followed by an unprecedented first interview with a sympathetic news outlet.

CHUKS. They are not going to listen to me.

LAURENCE. Of course they will. What's the point of blowing up a pipeline if there's no one there to report it?

CHUKS. Maybe they just like the boom.

LAURENCE. No way. No way. Are you with me?

CHUKS. No, my friend.

LAURENCE. Please.

CHUKS. *Wallahi!* Who do you think you are?

LAURENCE. Okay. How much is he paying you?

CHUKS. Two hundred thousand.

LAURENCE. What!

CHUKS. Two hundred K.

LAURENCE. I don't have that kind of money. I can do fifty, maximum.

CHUKS. Forget it.

Pause.

LAURENCE. I have another offer. Take him to do his interview. Take his money. I'll stick around here. Then when he's gone, take me to the boys and I'll give you another fifty thousand. That way we both get interviews, you get paid twice, everybody's happy.

CHUKS *is pondering this offer when* DAVE *returns.*

DAVE. Chuks, we should get going.

LAURENCE. Good idea, you should get moving.

DAVE. Yeah, we should.

LAURENCE. Clock's ticking.

DAVE eyes LAURENCE suspiciously.

DAVE. You heading back then?

LAURENCE. Haven't finished my drink yet.

Pause.

DAVE. Haven't finished mine either.

LAURENCE. Leave it. I'll buy you another back at the hotel.

DAVE sits back down at the table.

DAVE. I'll just put this one away. Might as well.

All three men drink in awkward silence.

Laurence.

LAURENCE. Yes.

DAVE. Did you cut a deal?

LAURENCE. What?

DAVE. Did you cut a fucking deal? Come to an arrangement. (*Points at* CHUKS.) With him?

LAURENCE. No, Dave. I can honestly say I didn't, no.

DAVE. Because we had more than a gentlemen's agreement.

LAURENCE. The contract's inked?

DAVE. Money has changed hands here, you understand?

LAURENCE. Absolutely.

DAVE. The arrangement is exclusive, unfortunately. I'd hate to think you were trying to undercut me.

LAURENCE. I'm hurt, Dave, that you'd think that.

DAVE (*to* CHUKS). We have a deal, right? You're not doing business with this man?

LAURENCE (*to* CHUKS). You're not doing business with me, are you?

DAVE (*to* CHUKS). Because I think you're an honest man.

LAURENCE (*to* CHUKS). You're an honest man, aren't you?

DAVE (*to* CHUKS). Aren't you?

LAURENCE (*to* CHUKS). Are you?

CHUKS *explodes out of his seat.*

CHUKS. You people are not serious! Jesus.

Pause.

I am finished with this nonsense. I have changed my mind. You know what is honest? We can drive around this place forty days and forty nights, but we will not find anybody. I honestly don't want to find them. Keep your money.

CHUKS *pulls out the wad of notes and holds it out to* DAVE.

Take it.

DAVE *does so, reluctantly.*

DAVE. Well, you fucked that up for me, Laurence.

CHUKS. It is good money, but you people are jokers. I don't want to deal with these boys. They are serious shit.

DAVE. So you do know them.

CHUKS. Yes. I know them, and they know me and my business. They have already warned me.

DAVE. Warned you that what?

CHUKS. They say I don' help you pressmen, don' get fat, don' chop the food you buy me.

DAVE. It's hot air.

CHUKS. No. You don't understand what I am telling you. Open your ears, eh? If I help you to find them, they will come back and find me. They will make trouble for me after you have already packed up your things and gone back to your five-star. No deal, no deal.

Pause.

You want to know what the boys said to me? You want to know? They showed me something. But the thing my eye see, my mouth no fit talk am.

DAVE. Try.

CHUKS. They showed me a picture they snapped. Of a man. This traitor betrayed the boys, so they beat the hell out of him. The blood was pouring. The man was dying. He begged the boys to take him to the hospital.

Pause.

So they put him in the boot of a car and they drove him to the hospital. When they reached there, they carried him out of the car and went inside. They took him to the mortuary. They opened one of the freezers, and they closed him inside. When he was still alive.

Pause.

Then the boys left the hospital. But nobody helped the man in the freezer, because the boys said 'don't help him'.

Pause.

I am not messing with the boys. They suspect me I am a traitor. They say I make too much cash from my business with you people. They think I take money left right and centre to open this bar.

CHUKS *waves an arm at the room.*

They ask which *oyinbos* I take money from next – the pipeline consortium?

Pause.

DAVE. So why'd you take my money?

DAVE *realises.*

To trick me? Drive me around on a tour of the north. And not find the boys. Waste my time. And charge me anyway, right?

Pause.

Take me to see the boys.

CHUKS. Did you not hear me?

DAVE. Take me, and I will take care of you. Get you out safe. Straight away. Move you out of the north. Down to Lagos.

CHUKS (*waves an arm at the room*). What about here?

DAVE. I'll get you a job as a driver. Want a new job?

LAURENCE. You've already got a driver.

DAVE (*to* LAURENCE). Yeah, I do. But you don't. You could do with a driver.

LAURENCE. I don't need a driver.

DAVE. Want to join forces on this one? You can come and do the interview with me. Seriously, Laurence. Let's do this.

LAURENCE. I don't need a driver. (*To* CHUKS.) The boys are right about you, aren't they?

CHUKS. What?

LAURENCE. You do take money from everyone. You were going to take ours, screw us two over, take me on a pointless tour of the north. And you know what? I'd guess you were going to get cash off the pipeline consortium at the same time.

CHUKS. What?

LAURENCE. I bet the consortium is paying you to keep journalists away from the militants.

CHUKS. That is a lie.

LAURENCE. If you don't take both me and my colleague here to see the boys, I'm going to put it about that you not only took money from me, you took consortium cash to spy on the boys.

DAVE. What are you talking about?

CHUKS. No. No, I did not take anything.

LAURENCE. It will be on the news tonight. In the papers tomorrow. A traitor. A consortium man. What could be worse than that? The boys will show you some love.

DAVE. Laurence…

CHUKS *indicates the door.*

CHUKS. You should go back to your hotel.

LAURENCE. I haven't paid.

CHUKS. No need.

LAURENCE. Go on. You pick.

CHUKS. What?

LAURENCE. Slap on the wrist for a small-time fixer or a traitor's head, rolling on the floor?

DAVE. Christ, Laurence.

LAURENCE. The boys might put you in the deep freeze.

DAVE. Stop it, Laurence.

LAURENCE. Chilled ice-cold.

Pause.

CHUKS (*quietly*). Okay, let's go. Let's go and find them.

LAURENCE. Great. Finally.

DAVE. No.

LAURENCE. Dave, please. We're just getting somewhere, mate. Want to come?

DAVE. No. (*To* CHUKS.) You don't have to go. Not if it will put you in danger.

LAURENCE. I'm putting down good money here.

LAURENCE *puts some cash on the table. He makes a 'help yourself' gesture to* CHUKS. *After a few seconds,* CHUKS *takes the money.*

(*To* DAVE.) You might want to throw in your fair share. I'm doing you a favour here too.

DAVE. Leave it alone, Laurence.

LAURENCE. Why should I?

DAVE. It's just fucking unethical.

LAURENCE. I just paid for the man's services in a business transaction. Fair and square. He's an entrepreneur.

DAVE. He's fucked.

CHUKS. If you people want to go, let's go.

DAVE (*to* CHUKS). You don't have to do this. He's just bluffing. He won't slander you.

LAURENCE. Fine, Dave. You can stay here then. We'll go and see the boys for my exclusive. Chuks?

LAURENCE *downs the rest of his beer and heads for the door.* CHUKS *prepares to follow him.* DAVE *stares forlornly at the table, fiddles with his satphone.*

DAVE. Wait.

CHUKS *and* LAURENCE *turn.*

DAVE *rummages in a pocket. He retrieves the wad of cash from earlier and hands it to* CHUKS, *who takes it in silence.* CHUKS *indicates the door.*

The two reporters go out, followed by their fixer.

Scene Six

Two airline seats, side by side. Not on a plane but somewhere outside. CHUKS *waits in one seat and* DAVE *in the other. An armed* MAN *sporting heavy weaponry, a balaclava, camouflage military fatigues and rubber flip-flops stands some way off. The shadows of unseen gunmen flit about.*

DAVE. It was Sierra Leone. Got trapped on the wrong side of the lines. This conscript was explaining the cuts of dog meat. The whole animal, he said that's called Peugeot 504. Or wait, wrong model, it was 404. So it follows, the head, that's the gearbox. To order a leg, you ask for the tyres. The head was headlights, hang on, no, that was the gearbox.

CHUKS. Stop telling me this.

DAVE. Said it made a good stew. I tried some, it was chewy, not bad though. Ever tried it?

DAVE *looks at the* MAN IN FLIP-FLOPS, *and then over his shoulder.*

How long's Laurence been in there?

CHUKS *shrugs.*

Maybe I should go and check.

CHUKS. I do not think that would be a good idea.

DAVE. No, you're right.

DAVE *looks around.*

Must be a hundred people live somewhere this size. Where'd they all go?

Pause.

Think they're hiding in the houses?

CHUKS. They have packed their things go.

DAVE. And the boys. One minute the place is teeming with them, the next... I don't like this, us being left alone. No one leaves you alone out here, ever.

DAVE *studies the* MAN IN FLIP-FLOPS.

Doesn't seem very friendly, does he?

CHUKS. No.

DAVE. He's staring at me.

CHUKS. Then stop looking at him.

DAVE. Red eyes.

CHUKS. Stop.

DAVE. Stoned maybe.

CHUKS. Stop looking at him.

DAVE. I should go in.

DAVE *stands. The* MAN IN FLIP-FLOPS *twitches, reaches for his gun.* CHUKS *grabs* DAVE*'s arm and pulls him back down into his seat.*

No, I'll wait here with you.

Pause.

He's been in there a while though, Laurence, hasn't he? Twenty minutes now? More. He was supposed to have ten, he's eating into my time.

DAVE *fiddles with the airline seats.*

This stuff used to be more fun.

CHUKS. Fun? How is that?

DAVE. You come out to these places. You're free. No commitments. Not like the people back home. Ten years later you realise you've no commitments 'cause no one gives a shit about you. Never be an old journalist. It's undignified.

DAVE *checks his watch*.

What did you say to get us in?

CHUKS. I said these are reasonable people. One is Dave and one is Laurence. They do not understand you. They want to understand you.

DAVE. That was it?

CHUKS. Yes.

> CHUKS *stops. The* MAN IN FLIP-FLOPS *has come within earshot.* CHUKS *acknowledges him.*

(*Cheery.*) Alhaji, how is it going, sir?

> *The* MAN IN FLIP-FLOPS *appears not to notice.*

DAVE (*feigns calm*). Who was your contact?

CHUKS. He was a friend of my cousin.

DAVE. What does your cousin do?

CHUKS. Gone to New York.

DAVE. To do what?

CHUKS. Study. I wrote to ask him to send me some things, a TV, but he didn't reply my letters.

> *The* MAN IN FLIP-FLOPS *is still there.* CHUKS *stands up and produces his phone.*

(*Cheery.*) Alhaji, sir, we should snap your photo together. Dave, come let us take a photo.

DAVE. Is this really necessary?

CHUKS. Come on, we are all friends here. A nice memento.

> DAVE *goes to stand by the* MAN IN FLIP-FLOPS. *The* MAN IN FLIP-FLOPS *strikes a pose with his weapon.* CHUKS *frames the shot.*

Looking good, good-looking.

> CHUKS *takes a photo of the absurd pair. The* MAN IN FLIP-FLOPS *wanders away.* DAVE *and* CHUKS *sit back down.*

That was a bad thing, just now, when I got out of the car. Today my contact he said 'no problem', last time it was a mistake when they were shooting. But these people are unreliable, they are trouble. One day they are saying one thing, the next day they are saying another thing. Who knows what they are smoking? Who knows what they are even thinking. I thought they were going to shoot me. You were just sitting in the car. You should have come out of the car with me, instead of only me standing there. They are not going to shoot you, after all.

DAVE. What are you talking about? They shot Jerome.

CHUKS. They were aiming for the car.

DAVE. Who knows where they were aiming? Sorry, but I don't think me getting out would have made any difference. Might have made things worse, actually.

CHUKS. So you were staying inside the car so that you could drive away quickly…

DAVE. That's not how it was.

CHUKS. Drive away quickly if they started shooting at me.

DAVE. Anyway, it's under the bridge, you handled it fine. And they seem to like Laurence's schtick. There's been no trouble.

CHUKS (*looks over shoulder*). Then what is he doing in there with that man all this time? He has been in there a long time now. He is probably provoking them. That your friend, he is a joker, he is a problem…

A sudden noise and both men look round. A second armed MAN *appears and walks in the direction of the first. He too is wearing a balaclava, along with mirrored aviator sunglasses, vest and worn trainers.*

DAVE *and* CHUKS' *heads track the* MAN IN MIRROR SHADES'*s passage across their field of vision, and stop when he stops. The armed men confer in low tones, and then the* MAN IN FLIP-FLOPS *walks off.*

DAVE. Look, I wasn't hiding in the car.

Pause.

You just seemed like the better man to open negotiations.

Pause.

And it's not like you can claim the moral high ground. You were planning on ripping me off.

CHUKS. What is 'ripping off'?

DAVE. Took money and you weren't planning on bringing me here at all. Cheating me.

CHUKS. Look, I provide an excellent service. That was a small small thing.

DAVE. It starts small.

CHUKS. No, it starts big. Mostly, I am the one who is cheated. Somebody opens a shop, they cheat me, gives me a job, doesn't pay me, starts a church and thieves the donations, police set up roadblocks, stop me and take take take.

Pause.

Mostly, I am the one they are cheating. When you are looking around, do you *see* that this is a rich country? Do you see it?

DAVE. Seems the boys agree with you.

CHUKS. The boys can be running around in the bush the whole time, blaming the foreigners. But the oil money is here, you understand me? Building villas in Lagos. They cheat me, I am not complaining, I will cheat it back. That is not politics, it is practicality.

DAVE. I'm not an oil company.

CHUKS. You expect me to be… what? One crooked guy in an honest world will win, but one honest guy in a crooked world, he is in trouble. The only sensible thing to do is to rise above one's situation. Play the game and play better.

DAVE. What if you lose?

CHUKS. It is better than to be eating dog meat.

LAURENCE *shows up, clutching his notebook.* DAVE *stands.*

DAVE. Is everything okay? How'd it go?

LAURENCE. Went great, Dave.

DAVE. You ate into my time.

LAURENCE. You're up.

DAVE *heads off.* LAURENCE *sits down in* DAVE*'s seat and looks around. He waves at the* MAN IN MIRROR SHADES. CHUKS *fixes his eyes on the ground.*

(*To* MAN IN MIRROR SHADES.) Hi!

He gives the figure a grin and a breezy thumbs up. The figure just stares back, impassive in his shades.

These guys are something. Some passionate people around here. Heated.

CHUKS. Is that so?

LAURENCE. Maybe I should go and talk to that one.

CHUKS. That is not a good idea.

LAURENCE. He's okay. Had a drink with him earlier.

LAURENCE *squints at the* MAN IN MIRROR SHADES.

At least, I think it was him.

CHUKS. Trouble dey sleep, una go wake am?

LAURENCE. Him in there. (*Indicates over his shoulder.*) He won't give his name. Not even a *nom de guerre.* Do you know his name?

CHUKS. No name. If you ask him, he will say his name is no name.

LAURENCE *gets out his dictaphone.*

What are you going to say?

LAURENCE. Just getting down some colour while I'm here.

CHUKS. Meaning what?

LAURENCE *dictates.*

LAURENCE. In the empty village, the gunmen shift uneasily. The dusty, arid expanse of the Sahel landscape stands testament to the vast distance the oil has been transported from where it was extracted in the sweltering mangrove swamps of the south. A gleaming iron snake...

CHUKS. What?

LAURENCE. The gleaming metal pipeline snakes its way across the horizon. The heat rises off its surface, the hot air shimmers and ripples, distorting the landscape. The great iron snake...

CHUKS. Iron snake?

LAURENCE. ... thrums in the background, a deep bass of low mechanical vibration.

CHUKS. It does not resemble a snake.

LAURENCE. Its cargo the most desirable of all, light sweet crude, destined to power the engines of the economies of distant destinations...

CHUKS. Also the material is aluminium.

LAURENCE. The boys are with us, always vigilant, watchful. The rough throng that met us when we arrived has melted away into the scrub.

CHUKS *looks around dubiously.*

CHUKS. They are over there.

LAURENCE. We sense a hundred hidden eyes on us.

CHUKS *snorts.*

In fact, only one lone fighter stands vigil now. His vest, dirty, his Nikes, torn...

CHUKS. It is Adidas.

LAURENCE. What?

CHUKS. His canvas. (*Laughs.*) Adidas.

LAURENCE *snaps off his dictaphone.*

LAURENCE. What's wrong with you?

CHUKS. Nothing.

LAURENCE. Why aren't you angry? At least these guys believe in something.

CHUKS. I believe in something.

LAURENCE. What?

CHUKS. Not getting involved.

LAURENCE. There are people down south been fighting the oil companies for decades. You know what's going on? You want them building pipelines through here now? Doesn't it bother you? As a northerner?

CHUKS. I am not from the north.

LAURENCE. You're not?

CHUKS. You cannot tell that from my name?

Pause.

North, south, it is how it is.

LAURENCE. No. No, forget that. Everywhere I go here, I seem to meet you. You know what? You're what's gone wrong. The worse it gets, the better it is for business, right?

DAVE *returns.*

That was quick.

DAVE. You're an insufferable little turd, Laurence.

LAURENCE. Dave.

DAVE. You ate into my time. Only got a couple of lines out of the grinning fucker, after all that.

LAURENCE. Too bad, Dave.

DAVE. And I thought you were getting knifed in there or something. You ate into my time.

LAURENCE. Guess he preferred talking to me.

A rumble starts up in the distance, along with a faint rat-a-tat of gunfire. The armed men confer.

What's that?

CHUKS. I don't know.

The armed men sprint off.

DAVE. Something's happening.

CHUKS. Let's go.

LAURENCE. Yes, let's go. You driving or riding in back?

CHUKS. It doesn't matter.

Scene Seven

*The bar, next day. There is an intermittent rumble as army trucks
pass by outside.* SARA *and* JEROME *burst in. They search
around, but there is only a packed bag on a table.*

SARA. Well, where is he?

JEROME. I don't know.

SARA. Is this the right place?

JEROME. Yeah.

SARA. What's it called again?

JEROME. Madam Hannah.

SARA. And you're sure it's the right place?

JEROME. I already said it was.

SARA. But you haven't been here before.

JEROME. No.

SARA. Madam Hannah?

JEROME. Yes.

SARA. Why would he call it that? He's called Chuks, isn't he?
  That's what you said.

JEROME. It's his daughter's name.

SARA. Madam?

JEROME. Hannah.

SARA. Maybe he's just gone out for a bit, down the road to get
  something. He didn't lock up.

JEROME. Friendly country.

SARA. We should just wait, don't you think?

JEROME. No way, we can't stay here.

  SARA *sits at a table. She leafs through some printouts.*

  Do you understand what's happening? This is a major
  mobilisation. It isn't regular army manoeuvres. They're
  moving out of town, they're going towards the pipeline.

SARA *takes off her jacket*.

It's curfew soon. We can't be out on the streets right now.
Let's go.

SARA. I want to speak to Chuks.

JEROME. What the hell for? You've seen the story. He already
took them, it's too late.

SARA. Does he live here too? Wonder where his daughter is.

JEROME. He's keeping his head down, like any sane person in
this town. We need to go. Now.

SARA *doesn't move*. JEROME *kicks the fridge in frustration*.

Look. Nothing good is about to happen. I'm out of here. I am
getting in the car and I am driving away.

SARA. You're leaving me here?

JEROME. Absolutely I'm leaving you.

SARA. Go then.

He doesn't. Her phone rings.

(*Into phone*.) Sara Maudsley.

Yes, I'm aware of the *Daily Post* story.

JEROME *opens the fridge*.

No, Jerome's the Regional Head of Communications. I'm only
a consultant.

She looks over at JEROME, *who is rummaging through the
fridge*.

He's currently in a strategy meeting.

I don't get the impression he's planning on coming out of the
meeting at this point, I have to admit. Okay, wait a moment.

SARA *thinks of a response*.

You can use this quote. Ready? There is no foundation to the
speculative allegations being made in the media.

We strongly refute the unfounded story in the *Post*, and would
like to make clear it is completely untrue that the consortium
is using heavy-handed tactics in relation to the trans-Saharan
pipeline.

We can't stop the military assault on the boys. We're not responsible for the actions of a sovereign government.

We are surprised that a supposedly reputable newspaper has allowed itself to become a mouthpiece for violent thugs.

JEROME *cracks open a beer.*

Okay – got it? We're not saying more than that at the present time.

She hangs up.

God. And it's only just broken.

JEROME. We can do this back at the hotel.

SARA. We're into damage limitation with the first story, but if there's more on the way maybe we can get on top of it, get the lawyers to make a few pre-emptive calls.

JEROME. What did London say?

SARA. Shares in consortium companies are tanking. Crude oil prices are pushing past the hundred-dollar-a-barrel mark. Prospect of long-term instability and security issues with the pipeline. How do you think we should play this?

JEROME *shrugs.*

Why don't you start by rereading the story?

SARA *gives* JEROME *the printouts.*

JEROME. We will fight them with or without shoes. Good quote.

SARA. Jerome, that's not helpful.

JEROME. I've been cut out of the loop. You going to tell me why we're really here?

SARA. Depends.

JEROME. On what, exactly?

SARA. I'm starting to question your reliability.

JEROME. Excuse me?

SARA. It was you, wasn't it? You helped them. You sent Dave to your old fixer.

JEROME. What are you talking about?

SARA. You're old friends.

JEROME. What is this?

SARA. I saw you whispering.

JEROME. Look, whatever. If I say it was me, can we leave?

SARA. No, Jerome. No, we can't bloody leave. You seem to have forgotten you're not a journalist any more.

JEROME (*snaps*). No, I'm not a journalist. I never forget I'm not a journalist. I never forget I sold out for *this*.

Pause.

SARA. So that's it.

Pause.

I read what you wrote. After you were shot. It was angry. I guess you took the job to get your own back, and now you're regretting it. I know why you handed the reporters the fixer.

JEROME. You do?

SARA. To prove you're not some corporate tool. Because what you think you are is some kind of… adventurer. This is a big playground, and you're suddenly on the other side of the fence from your friends and they're all pointing at you. You want to play but you can't, and it's killing you.

JEROME *just stares.*

We're not perfect, we've made mistakes, but we're committed to this country. We'll be here when your friends have long since got bored and gone home.

JEROME. *You'll* be here.

JEROME *walks out. A car drives off.* SARA *flicks through the printouts again. Some time passes before the bag catches her eye. She goes over, unzips it and looks inside.* CHUKS *enters.*

SARA. You're Chuks.

CHUKS. Who wants to know?

SARA. I'm Sara.

CHUKS. From the consortium.

SARA. You noticed.

CHUKS. I hear many things. You should not come here, outside is dangerous.

SARA. Yes, I know.

CHUKS. Somebody may see you here. You have to go now.

SARA. I wanted to ask you something.

CHUKS. Who does not?

CHUKS *retrieves the bag.*

You also want to meet the boys.

SARA. No. Definitely not.

CHUKS. Then what?

SARA. A message. I need you to take a message. You're the only person we know of that's made direct contact.

CHUKS. But you are the consortium.

SARA. I suppose I am.

CHUKS. What message?

SARA. Will you take it?

CHUKS *laughs.*

You'd be doing a public service.

CHUKS. Lady, do I look like a public servant to you?

SARA. It might help to stop... (*Indicates the rumbling outside.*) all this.

CHUKS. How is that?

SARA. Will you take it? I know the situation is difficult. You don't have to. But obviously, as an agent...

CHUKS. Of the consortium.

SARA. There'd be a substantial fee in it. You'd be a man of considerable means.

CHUKS. I will give your request all due consideration.

He checks through the bag.

SARA. You're leaving.

CHUKS. I am going down to the south.

SARA. What about your daughter?

CHUKS. How do you know about my daughter?

SARA. I hear things too.

CHUKS. She is staying with her auntie, it is okay. I will send for her after. But at this moment I need to get petrol for two days of driving. Nobody has, everywhere is queues.

He puts the bag down.

What is your message?

Pause.

SARA. There's an idea being mooted.

CHUKS. Idea?

SARA. We will pay them.

CHUKS. Pay who?

SARA. The boys.

CHUKS. Pay them for what?

SARA. Security. The consortium will pay them to provide security along the entire northern section of the pipeline.

CHUKS. Lady, *joke na joke*.

SARA. They have considerable experience with the pipeline. They know it well. Best candidates for the job.

CHUKS. How much?

SARA. Half a million, potentially.

CHUKS *laughs*.

Not naira. Dollars.

CHUKS *stops laughing*.

We thought perhaps you could put out some feelers. Before the military do something... excessive.

CHUKS. Let me understand. You want to employ the boys who are blowing up the pipeline to provide security to prevent themselves from blowing up the pipeline?

SARA. Effectively, yes.

CHUKS. These boys are crazy people.

SARA. If it works, our bunch of crazy people.

CHUKS. *Kai!* Wonders will never cease. What kind of person could conceive such a thing? It is really something.

SARA. You think it will work?

CHUKS. Really something.

SARA. You think they'll be amenable?

CHUKS. When it comes to money, who is not amenable? (*Laughs.*) Oh. Oh. Amazing. Incredible. So this is how it is done. I am only an amateur!

SARA. They might have ideological objections.

CHUKS. That is true.

SARA. You'll do it?

Pause.

You can sell it to them?

CHUKS. I can sell anything. Anything. This is Chuks.

SARA. It might be risky.

CHUKS. Is this not what I do? God has brought me this far. I went to the boys and am I not still here? One more time so then I can go anywhere. A man of considerable means! New York. Take my daughter. Correct her leg. Visit my cousin. I think he will be surprised to see me after all this time. Maybe I will drive a taxi. To start, then open a business. A Nigerian restaurant. Buy a TV. Sixty-four inch. Wear nice shoes. Become a millionaire. Marry some American wife. Success, eh. Success. US!

SARA. Hotdogs.

CHUKS. Money.

SARA. Cars.

CHUKS. Guns.

CHUKS *deflates. Stops.*

SARA. What is it?

CHUKS. I cannot deliver your message.

SARA. But what you just said…

CHUKS. It will not happen.

Pause.

SARA. I'm sorry you feel that way. I hope you'll reconsider.

CHUKS *doesn't respond.* SARA *digs out a piece of paper and hands it over.*

Here. I put the main points down.

CHUKS *screws the paper up into a ball without reading it. Hands it back.* SARA *holds it for a moment, then goes to* CHUKS's *bag. She opens it, sticks the ball of paper inside, then zips it back up again.*

In case you change your mind.

SARA *gathers up her things.*

I have to get back to the hotel. I seem to have lost my transportation.

Pause.

CHUKS. I will carry you.

SARA. Perhaps we can talk more on the way.

CHUKS. Talk all you want.

Scene Eight

The hotel lobby. It is late. CHUKS *is lying on the couch, his bag close by. The* PORTER *enters, keys in hand. He spots* CHUKS.

PORTER. What are you doing here?

CHUKS. You don't have eyes?

PORTER. Afraid no catch you? The curfew has started. *Soja man* is everywhere.

CHUKS. So I have to stay.

PORTER. You should go.

CHUKS. It is not safe in my place. I was going to the south but I could not get petrol.

PORTER. Go, eh?

CHUKS. Did you see outside? It is shoot on sight.

PORTER. Come on.

CHUKS. It is late.

PORTER. So you should go quick quick.

CHUKS. *Ah-ah*.

PORTER. What are you even doing here? You don' reach payday already. You took the pressmen to the boys.

CHUKS. Yes.

PORTER. Chuks. Why did you do that?

CHUKS. Is it not what I do?

PORTER. Those boys. *Kai!* And you are okay, yes?

CHUKS. Of course.

PORTER. Go, eh? You cannot sleep in this place.

CHUKS. Stay, talk.

PORTER. I have to work.

CHUKS. You have a beer delivery tomorrow?

PORTER. Gulder. Maybe Star also.

CHUKS. Keep a crate of Star for me.

PORTER. If I keep it, then you should go now.

CHUKS. How was the interview?

PORTER. He gave me the job.

CHUKS. Seriously? I am looking at the new hotel barman?

PORTER. Yes.

CHUKS. Congratulations.

PORTER. Thank you.

CHUKS. You see. You were correct. I told you the manager will dupe you. But he has promoted you. What do I know? I don' sit in this place too long.

He slaps the PORTER *on the back.*

I am happy for you. Very happy. Well done.

PORTER. What is this? Are you not supposed to tell me I am worthless?

CHUKS. You are worthless, my friend!

PORTER. Begin go, eh.

CHUKS. Come on, sit down.

PORTER. Begin go.

JEROME *enters. The* PORTER *sees him and leaves.* JEROME *heads towards the exit for a smoke.*

CHUKS. There is a curfew.

JEROME. It's you. Where have you been?

CHUKS. Around.

JEROME. How were the boys? They seem popular these days. Things keep going like this, you'll have to lay on a bus.

CHUKS. Ah, Jerome, let me explain…

JEROME. Doesn't matter. I'm out of here.

CHUKS. You are leaving the country?

JEROME. I quit the consortium. New suit don't always fit right, know what I'm saying?

CHUKS. So you are a journalist again.

JEROME. No. Some things, you can't go back. The corporates think I'm a journo and the journos think I'm a corporate.

CHUKS. So what do you do?

JEROME. Take a vacation. See my folks. Go someplace.

Pause.

Got to hand it to you. The boys giving interviews. What d'you know?

CHUKS. Everything cost.

JEROME. You don't say.

JEROME *goes out.* CHUKS *lies back down and goes to sleep.*

DAVE, LAURENCE, SARA *and* JEROME *enter. They pace about, voices overlapping as they speak on their phones.*

LAURENCE. Copytaker? Copytaker? I need to file my follow-up please. Are you ready?

JEROME. Royal Excelsior Palace? Yeah, I'd like a room for the day after tomorrow.

SARA. No, I'm afraid you can't speak to Jerome. He's no longer with the consortium.

LAURENCE (*dictating slowly and clearly*). Last night the situation appeared to be spinning out of control as militants vowed to step up their campaign. Point, par.

JEROME. Is that the only room you've got? I wanted something a bit bigger.

SARA. Jerome left at short notice I'm afraid. He's spending more time with his, um…

JEROME. What's the difference between the deluxe and the suite?

LAURENCE (*dictating*). The pipeline fire has now been burning for several consecutive days. Point, par.

JEROME. No, not the suite, that's too much. A deluxe is fine. Have you got a swimming pool?

SARA. I've been seconded in as Acting Regional Director of Communications for the consortium.

LAURENCE (*dictating*). The militants claim the consortium is pressuring the Government to send in the army as part of a crackdown. Point, new par.

JEROME. Is the room air-conditioned?

DAVE. No. No no no.

SARA. You'll be dealing with me now Jerome's gone.

DAVE. You didn't run my story.

JEROME. You want the deposit now? I'll give you my credit-card number.

LAURENCE (*dictating*). Two army battalions are rumoured to have entered the area in the past forty-eight hours alone as tension escalates. Point, par.

DAVE. You didn't run it!

JEROME. 0687-3495-6000-5555.

SARA. Yes, of course. Let's have lunch as soon as I get back to Lagos. Whenever that is.

LAURENCE. Can you read that last bit back to me?

The hubbub dies down as JEROME, SARA, DAVE *and* LAURENCE *disperse. It is dead quiet for some time.*

A MAN *in a tracksuit comes in from the direction of the hotel reception and lingers near the door. He watches* CHUKS *for some time before going over to touch him.* CHUKS *jumps. He recognises the visitor.*

CHUKS. Welcome.

CHUKS stands up.

Welcome, please sit.

The TRACKSUIT MAN *takes a seat and smiles at* CHUKS.

Let me get you something.

CHUKS goes out to the hotel reception. He returns with a beer and hands it over, then stands near the TRACKSUIT MAN's chair.

MAN. You are surprised.

CHUKS. No. No, welcome.

The TRACKSUIT MAN *drinks.*

I was stranded here. The curfew.

Pause.

MAN. I went to Madam Hannah to find you. That is a nice place. *Oga.* Big man.

CHUKS. I try my best.

MAN. God don' butter your bread.

CHUKS. I am working hard.

MAN. Well done.

Pause.

You should buy some pictures to put on the wall. In Madam Hannah.

CHUKS. Eh?

MAN. Something like flowers or a nice beach. A lake. You know what I am saying, with the mountains in the back. Somewhere with no people. Beautiful.

CHUKS. I will organise it.

MAN. Seriously?

CHUKS. Of course. I respect your advice. We are friends.

MAN. Is that so?

CHUKS. Yes.

MAN. You have many friends.

CHUKS. I have a bar. Many people come there.

MAN. Is everybody your friend?

CHUKS. No. Of course not.

The TRACKSUIT MAN *laughs, then takes a leisurely swig of his beer.* CHUKS *fidgets.*

MAN. You have a very big mouth.

CHUKS *shakes his head.*

But your ears are too small.

CHUKS. No way.

The TRACKSUIT MAN *puts his drink down on the table with a bump.* CHUKS *jumps.*

MAN. Those pressmen. Why do you like them? The *oyinbo*. And that boy, the one that talks too much and wants to tell everybody the truth.

CHUKS. I don't like them.

MAN. The truth is that he gave me a headache from talking too fast.

CHUKS. He is a motormouth.

MAN. That story that he wrote, I read it on the internet. He said I am the… (*Struggles to recall the quote.*) 'vanguard of the resistance to the new colonialism'. (*Laughs.*) What do you think about that?

CHUKS. I don't know…

MAN. The boy is an idiot.

CHUKS. You are correct, he is an idiot.

MAN. But I have to confess, he is also very intelligent.

CHUKS. Yes, very intelligent.

MAN. He told us some constructive things. He gave our organisation advice on the importance of – what did he say – getting our message out.

CHUKS. Your message?

MAN. Our side of the story. We now have a committee for the formulation of media strategy.

CHUKS. A committee?

MAN. I am the chairman. We plan to convene once a week. On Thursdays.

CHUKS. Today is Thursday.

MAN. And it is a good day for a meeting. But this week we had to postpone it. I came here to visit you instead.

CHUKS. You see. You have a committee. So everything is satisfactory.

MAN. How is that so? We told you not to bring the pressmen. You did not listen to us. We shoot one, so the next time you bring two.

Pause.

Why do you allow them to be using you?

CHUKS. I am using them.

MAN. You dey sit in hotel bar with the prostitutes waiting for the *oyinbo* men to come for you. 'Yes, sir, no, sir, please, sir, take me, sir.'

The TRACKSUIT MAN *points at* CHUKS.

Whose side are you on?

CHUKS. I am not on any side.

MAN. With us your people or with those your friends?

CHUKS. It is business.

MAN. You have to take a side.

CHUKS. I don't quarrel with anybody. I am neutral. I am Switzerland.

MAN. Let me explain something to you. Every action we are taking here we are doing it for you. If we drive these greedy pipeline companies away, stop them transporting the oil through here, send a message to this useless Government, do you not benefit?

Pause.

CHUKS. Yes.

MAN. And you are not grateful? So who do you side with?

CHUKS (*quietly*). With you.

MAN. You are corrupt.

CHUKS (*forgets himself*). What am I supposed to do? When everything is stinking like shit, you think only me I will smell like perfume?

The TRACKSUIT MAN *is surprised.*

The smell of oil dey draw you. That fire, that big fire that don' bring all the pressmen running up here from Lagos. Everybody they were saying you were exploding the pipeline for politics. But was the whole thing not an accident? Were you not tapping the oil? Liberating the oil for the black market. To sell it. Is that not the truth? Then one stupid person sparked the fire. Boom!

The TRACKSUIT MAN *stands.*

MAN. We are not thieves. You don't respect our movement? You don't respect us?

CHUKS *half-reaches out to try and calm the* TRACKSUIT MAN.

CHUKS. No, no. Wait. I am very respectful. You want to tell your side of the story. So I helped you to do that, eh?

After a moment, the TRACKSUIT MAN *sits back down.*

Sorry. Let me tell you my situation.

CHUKS *kneels by the* TRACKSUIT MAN.

One day I was in the market and I saw a big crowd. One pressman was there asking for somebody to help him interpret. He was asking people what do they think about the Government. I said I don't know anything about politics, he said no problem. So I helped him. This person likes the Government, that one doesn't like. One hour we were there. When I finished he gave me his card.

Pause.

That was by chance. He recommended me to his friends, so every time they come to the north they are looking for Chuks. Whether I like it or not, they come.

MAN. And you cannot stop.

CHUKS. If I do not help these people, then somebody else will take the money. You want your fair share, I want mine. They need me, I am important to them. They are coming to Africa looking for bad things, horror film. I can give them the cinema.

MAN. You give them a bad image of this country.

CHUKS. You think it is *me* who does that?

MAN. Who else?

Something occurs to CHUKS. *He rummages in a pocket.*

CHUKS. My daughter, five years old.

CHUKS *produces a picture and hands it to the* TRACKSUIT MAN.

My daughter.

The TRACKSUIT MAN *studies the picture.*

She is very sick. She has polio. Look at it – you see the legs?

CHUKS *mimes a bending action with his hands.*

The legs don' bend make K.

MAN. *Kai!* That is terrible. Where is she?

Pause.

CHUKS. I sent her away.

Pause.

A long time now. She is living with my sister. I send them some small-small cash every week to help them. I am very reliable.

The TRACKSUIT MAN *returns the picture to* CHUKS.

MAN. So we are here.

CHUKS. Yes.

MAN. I came to ask you support the movement.

CHUKS. I don't know anything about politics.

MAN. Practical support. The pressmen paid cash for you to bring them to find us.

CHUKS. Only some small-small dash…

MAN. Time for repayment.

Pause.

CHUKS. You want money.

The TRACKSUIT MAN *nods.* CHUKS *laughs with sudden relief at the demand, pulls himself together. He gets to his feet rapidly.*

You came for money. Only money? My friend. What do you need?

MAN. We need to buy many things.

CHUKS. I can help you with that.

MAN. Toyota pick-ups second-hand, quality boots. A new tanker.

CHUKS. They cost.

MAN. It is exactly as you said. We have to tap some oil from the pipeline, sell it on the black market to finance the struggle. But it is not enough, everybody must make a contribution.

CHUKS. Of course.

MAN. I will agree something with you. In future, if you bring these people to us, we will talk to them. Whatever they like. And then we will take a percentage of the money that they give to you for our movement.

CHUKS. What?

MAN. Commission.

    CHUKS *puts his hands up*.

CHUKS. Okay, okay.

MAN. How much did those ones pay?

CHUKS. They only dashed me three thousand naira.

MAN. Come on.

CHUKS. Seriously.

    The TRACKSUIT MAN *shakes his head and drinks*.

    I will give you fifty per cent commission.

MAN. Too low.

CHUKS. It is a very good rate. I already gave the remainder of the money to my family, to my daughter.

    The TRACKSUIT MAN *drinks*.

    Cash one thousand five hundred now.

    CHUKS *pulls out some money from his pocket and hands it over*.

    You and the boys, welcome to Madam Hannah any time. Free beers, whatever you want.

MAN. Thank you.

CHUKS. We can do some deals in future.

MAN. You see, everybody is happy now.

CHUKS. Of course. We are all in the same game.

MAN (*laughs*). Business is everything with you.

CHUKS. Everything is good for business.

The TRACKSUIT MAN *pockets the money.*

MAN. Thank you, my friend.

CHUKS. Any time, any time.

Pause.

By the way…

MAN. Yes?

CHUKS *hesitates a moment, then goes ahead.*

CHUKS. I heard about something that may be of interest to you.

MAN. What is that?

CHUKS. A business opportunity. I have the particulars.

CHUKS *goes to his bag. Rummages out the screwed-up note* SARA *gave him and hands it over. The* TRACKSUIT MAN *reads.*

MAN. This is very interesting.

CHUKS. You see!

MAN. Very interesting. I must think about it.

CHUKS. Of course, of course.

The TRACKSUIT MAN *moves to the door.* CHUKS *starts to see him out, but instead of going outside, the* TRACKSUIT MAN *stops where he is and stares at* CHUKS.

MAN. Let's go.

CHUKS. Go to where?

The TRACKSUIT MAN *hits* CHUKS *without warning, knocking him to the floor. After a few moments,* CHUKS *looks up at the* TRACKSUIT MAN. *The* TRACKSUIT MAN *clicks his fingers and then points to the door.* CHUKS *gets to his feet slowly and goes out.*

The TRACKSUIT MAN *moves to follow* CHUKS *when the unfinished beer on the table catches his eye. He goes back to get his beer, then leaves the lobby.*

Scene Nine

Morning. The hotel lobby. SARA *sits on the couch. The* PORTER *picks up empty bottles.*

PORTER. Can I get you anything, madam?

SARA. You're… the porter.

PORTER. Yes, madam. No.

SARA. No?

PORTER. I am the barman. I was promoted.

SARA. Congratulations.

Pause.

Are you a friend of Chuks?

PORTER. Chuks?

SARA. He hangs around here sometimes.

PORTER. He was not allowed. To be hanging around.

SARA. You know him then.

PORTER. No.

SARA. No?

PORTER. Yes. I saw him sometimes.

SARA. Do you know where he is?

PORTER. Is he not here?

SARA. No. I was hoping he'd be back. If you see him, please tell him my offer's still open.

PORTER. I am sure he will come. He is fantastic. He does not fear anything. Not like me.

She smiles.

SARA. What's your name?

PORTER. Isa.

SARA. You should get in some gin.

PORTER. What?

SARA. For the bar. You're the barman, you say. The guests would love you for it. I'd love you for it.

PORTER. You are not going to the airport, madam?

SARA. Sara. I'm going to be staying up here a while. Longer than I thought. Monitoring the situation. A few weeks probably, before I can get back to Lagos.

PORTER. I will try and get gin.

SARA. It'd be just like a Lagos hotel, one of the big ones. Except in Lagos this place would be full.

PORTER. Yes.

SARA. Pretty dead now, this, here.

PORTER. It is the situation.

SARA. It's so empty with that lot gone. But I'm tired of the battles. People are so unreasonable, don't you think?

PORTER. They look, they don't want to see.

SARA. You're right, Isa. You know, I'll be back in the fray soon enough. And it's good to be out of the compound for a spell. Least up here it's dry heat, sweat dries off, just a bit of salt on the skin.

Pause.

Anyway, I'm sure you can find gin somewhere. Get your elusive friend Chuks to fix you up.

The PORTER *stares at her.*

What is it?

PORTER. He cannot arrange it.

The PORTER *sits.*

I saw Chuks.

SARA. When?

PORTER. There was trouble outside. But...

Pause.

Somebody came into here.

SARA. Oh?

PORTER. One of the boys. He came here. In the night.

He's really got her attention now.

He was wearing nice shoes. Adidas. He said, 'Let me in.' I said, 'It's late, the bar is closed.' This man, he was searching for Chuks. Chuks was sleeping inside here. He wanted to enter. I opened the door for him.

Pause.

It was the second time that this man was coming here. Two times yesterday. The first time he said that I should telephone him if I saw Chuks, he said he would dash me ten thousand naira. I was afraid. Last night…

Pause.

I telephoned the man.

Pause.

He dashed me the naira.

He pulls out some cash and pushes it at SARA.

I did not even want this. Please take it. I don't want it. The man he took Chuks away.

SARA. Here?

SARA stands.

They came in *here*?

Scene Ten

Two aircraft seats, side by side. LAURENCE *sits in one, toying with his headphones.*

DAVE *walks up, bag in one hand, ticket stub in the other. He looks around for his seat. He finds it next to* LAURENCE's.

LAURENCE. Shit.

DAVE *casts about for another seat. No luck. He sits down and fastens his seatbelt.* LAURENCE *puts on his headphones and shuts his eyes.*

STEWARDESS (*over speaker*). Ladies and gentlemen, welcome on board this flight from Lagos to London. We're just awaiting clearance right now. We'll be serving dinner shortly after take-off and I'd like to remind passengers that they will be able to choose from a wide selection of beers, wines and spirits.

DAVE pulls out a can of beer he has brought with him and pops the top. Pulls out another and pushes it at LAURENCE.

LAURENCE. Nah.

DAVE. How's it going?

LAURENCE takes his headphones off.

LAURENCE. What?

DAVE. All right?

LAURENCE. Fine.

DAVE. Holiday?

LAURENCE. No.

DAVE. You're going back?

LAURENCE. Yeah. Got a staff job back in London.

DAVE. That was quick. Congratulations.

LAURENCE. Thanks.

DAVE. Not stopping then.

LAURENCE. No.

DAVE. 'Pipeline in Peril' went down well.

LAURENCE. Oh. Yeah. Page five. Then page three the next day, and a big colour feature for the Saturday magazine.

DAVE. That's a good show.

Pause.

Mine too.

LAURENCE. Great.

DAVE. That's all good, then. Everyone's happy.

LAURENCE. Yeah.

LAURENCE puts his headphones back on. ·

DAVE. Actually, your stories got a better show than mine. I just did the one.

LAURENCE *nods without looking at* DAVE.

It got spiked. They needed the space for another story that came in. Late breaker. Some bit of fluff.

Pause.

Still. You wrote yours up better. Crunchier. Snappier. More... colourful.

LAURENCE. Look, do you mind?

DAVE. Sorry.

Pause.

They've cut my retainer. I'm done. Home-time.

Pause.

He's dead.

LAURENCE *pulls the headphones off.*

LAURENCE. What's that?

DAVE. Dead.

LAURENCE. Who?

DAVE. Chuks.

LAURENCE *looks closely at* DAVE.

LAURENCE. What are you talking about?

DAVE *drinks his beer.*

He was fine. It worked out fine. Boys were fine about it. Everyone got paid and was happy.

DAVE. He's disappeared.

LAURENCE. What are you talking about? Disappeared, dead. Different.

DAVE. Not round here.

LAURENCE. Where'd you hear that?

DAVE. He vanished and didn't come back. The bar's still there, and his things not touched.

LAURENCE. The boys were fine about it. Fine.

DAVE. You reckon?

LAURENCE. It was tense at the start, for sure, when we pull up and they're swinging their AKs and that. But he breaks the ice with them, sorts it, you know? He says, 'Hear these guys out before you shoot.' And I sell it to them, convince them we're worth talking to, I'm good at that, and then it's relaxed from thereon in and they put the guns away. They're joking and he's laughing with them and they are fine. They shoot their mouths off and they pose for pics with their AKs, and we all have a drink together and talk to the man with shit shoes and go home. He sorted it and he's okay.

Pause.

That's what happened, right?

Pause.

Fuck. Fuck.

DAVE. Why are you getting so worked up now?

LAURENCE. Worked up? I'm not worked up. I'm fine. He's probably just visiting relatives or something. Lying low for a while.

DAVE. Guess so.

LAURENCE *puts on his headphones and shuts his eyes. He takes the headphones off again.*

LAURENCE. It was a good story. Got the consortium on the back foot, got people to look closer at the pipeline, at the boys. It changed the state of play.

DAVE. Nothing changes.

LAURENCE. It stopped the crackdown. Consortium didn't want it – it didn't look good. Put pressure on the Government to stand the troops down. Things are calmer now.

DAVE. That wasn't because of the story.

LAURENCE. Course it was.

DAVE. I heard the consortium reached some sort of… accommodation with the boys.

LAURENCE. Accommodation?

DAVE. A financial accommodation.

LAURENCE. Who told you that?

DAVE. Just a rumour.

LAURENCE. Boys wouldn't take money from the consortium.

DAVE. Wouldn't they? The fires have stopped.

Pause.

LAURENCE. It was the press coverage calmed things down.

DAVE. Fine. Okay. Must have been the coverage. Your story did get a good show. Page five, you said?

LAURENCE. You want to make a difference, sometimes you've got to take a risk.

DAVE *doesn't respond.*

Nah. People read that story.

DAVE. They didn't read mine.

LAURENCE*'s headphones go back on.*

I took him out there for nothing.

LAURENCE. Will you shut up, please?

STEWARDESS (*over speaker*). Ladies and gentlemen, we do apologise, it appears we may be held on the tarmac for some time longer. I'm informed it may be up to an hour. But we'll keep you up to date and hopefully we'll be on our way.

DAVE. Soon as someone gets paid.

Pause.

Bad that it should happen like that, though. Wish you hadn't pushed it.

LAURENCE. Me?

DAVE. Yes. He'd never have taken us if you hadn't barrelled so far over the line.

LAURENCE. The line?

DAVE. You made it happen.

LAURENCE. And now things are happening for me, but not for you. Is that it, Dave? Yeah, I pushed it. How else do you get anything to happen round here? You push and you pull. You dash and bribe. You scratch a few backs if you need to. Push harder. That's how it works, isn't it?

DAVE. I guess so.

LAURENCE pretends to sleep. Eventually he pulls the headphones off again.

LAURENCE. How is this my fault anyway? You were there, tagged along. Did what you had to.

DAVE. No.

LAURENCE. Just like me.

DAVE. Not like you.

LAURENCE. Dangerman.

DAVE. No one died before.

LAURENCE. Feeling bad, Dave?

Pause.

Seems like everyone round here wants a percentage, so I'll give you one. Ten per cent my fault, ten per cent yours, okay? And eighty per cent his liability. That's the fixer's final cut.

DAVE *stares.*

Two-faced misery-merchant taking money with each hand. Corrupt, just like everything else in this place. Everyone taking, taking the money, grabbing the cash, no wonder it's all in the shit. That's the truth. He had it coming. He must have known it.

STEWARDESS (*over speaker*). Just while we wait I'll let you know what weather to expect at the other end. It's pretty cold and rainy in London at the moment, and the temperature on landing will be a few degrees above freezing.

DAVE. Ten per cent?

LAURENCE. These things happen.

Loud roar of jet engines.

The End.

Glossary

abeg: please

akara: fried bean balls

don': shortened form of 'done', means that something *has* happened

'Kai!': an exclamation

'Him chop, you chop': 'He gets a cut, you get a cut'

Inshallah: If God wills it

'Joke na joke': 'A joke is a joke, but…'

maitatsine: religious riot

mammy water: a mermaid-like spirit (also *Mami Wata*)

moimoi: steamed bean pudding

'Monkey dey work, baboon dey chop': 'The little people work, and the elite benefit'

oga: boss

Oyinbo: Westerner

par / pars: journo-speak for paragraph/s

'Sai gobe': 'Till tomorrow'

sannu: hello

soja man: soldier

'Trouble dey sleep, una go wake am?': 'Let sleeping dogs lie'

wahala: trouble

wallahi: I swear

Fixer was first presented as part of the HighTide Festival 2009, at The Cut, Halesworth, Suffolk, on 27 April 2009, produced by Samuel Hodges and Steven Atkinson. The cast (in order of appearance) was as follows:

JEROME	Todd Boyce
DAVE	Roger Evans
PORTER	Tunji Falana
SARA	Rae Hendrie
TRACKSUIT MAN	Clive Llewellyn
LAURENCE	Chiké Okonkwo
CHUKS	Israel Oyelumade

Director	Nathan Curry
Designer	takis
Lighting Designer	Matt Prentice
Sound Designer	Steven Mayo
Voice	John Tucker
Dramaturge	Sam Hodges
Casting	Camilla Evans
Assistant Director	Joe Murphy

A Nick Hern Book

Fixer first published in Great Britain in 2011 as a paperback original by Nick Hern Books Limited, 14 Larden Road, London W3 7ST, in association with Oval House Theatre, London

Fixer copyright © 2011 Lydia Adetunji

Lydia Adetunji has asserted her right to be identified as the author of this work

Cover image: weareasilia.com
Cover design: Ned Hoste, 2H

Typeset by Nick Hern Books, London
Printed in Great Britain by CLE Print Ltd, St Ives, Cambs PE27 3LE

A CIP catalogue record for this book is available from the British Library

ISBN 978 1 84842 064 9